THE NORSE TRADITION

a beginner's guide

THE NORSE TRADITION

 a beginner's guide

PETE JENNINGS

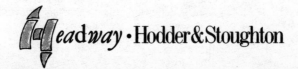

Order queries: please contact Bookpoint Ltd, 39 Milton Park, Abingdon, Oxon
OX14 4TD. Telephone: (44) 01235 400414, Fax: (44) 01235 400454. Lines are
open from 9.00–6.00, Monday to Saturday, with a 24-hour message answering
service. Email address: orders@bookpoint.co.uk

British Library Cataloguing in Publication Data
A catalogue record for this title is available from The British Library

ISBN 0 340 72082 4

First published 1998
Impression number 10 9 8 7 6 5 4 3 2 1
Year   2003 2002 2001 2000 1999 1998

Typeset by Transet Limited, Coventry, England.
Printed in Great Britain for Hodder & Stoughton Educational, a division of Hodder
Headline plc, 338 Euston Road, London NW1 3BH by Cox and Wyman Limited,
Reading, Berks.

To all who have taught and influenced me, including my friends in Odinshof, The Pagan Federation and my wife Sue.

The front cover shows the prow of a Viking ship, symbolising the Vikings' adventurous, pioneering spirit. May you adopt the brave demeanour of that dragon as you explore the magical worlds of Yggdrasil.

CONTENTS

WHAT IS THE NORSE TRADITION?

The Norse Tradition is a vibrant, living current within the multitude of spiritual paths of Paganism. It has more than one definition, but is generally agreed to be the original, natural folk religion of North Europeans of Teutonic origins. Those traditions come in a multitude of guises, from the temple dwellers at Uppsala, Sweden, to the fiercely independent Icelandic Gothi and Volva roles and on to the Danish and Saxon settlers and invaders of Britain. Although these forms may be separated by time and distance, they have a common thread of revering nature and acknowledging a multitude of goddesses as well as gods.

Of course, the Celts were doing comparable things in the same geographic area. It can be argued that the Romans' classification of tribes as either Celtic or Teutonic was purely arbitrary and that our modern mania for attributing a people to one 'pure' race or another would not have meant much at the time. However, the Celts have developed along a separate path, so let us concentrate on those who share some Teutonic words in their speech and some common mythology within their culture. It is this rich and colourful mythology which forms the basis for the Norse Tradition.

The Norse Tradition, sometimes called Odinism (after its chief God Odin), sometimes Northern Tradition (as in Northern Europe) or Asatru (from words meaning 'a faith in the Gods') is attractive today for many of the reasons for which it was followed long ago. It appeals to free thinkers and independent people who want a very direct and straightforward way of expressing their spirituality. It can be described as 'Paganism in your face!', and that directness either attracts or repels people, according to their nature. Unlike many

modern Pagan paths it has no formal degree structure, no universally recognised authoritative figures and no revered texts. Such a situation means that modern practitioners have to think out and do most things for themselves. Its evidence is firmly rooted within Northern European culture and people with Anglo Saxon or Danish names and origins are likely to be drawn into a feeling of 'belonging' or 'coming home' to a set of beliefs that gave us so many place names and even some of the days of the week, for example, Thursday from Thor's day. If you live in the UK it is likely that you are quite close to a Viking age archaeological site, such as Jorvik, the old Danish capital at York. If that, or the sight of the treasures from the Anglo Saxon burials at Sutton Hoo, Suffolk (kept in the British Museum) stir you, then a Northern Tradition path might be worth exploring.

A reconstruction of the Sutton Hoo helmet

Of course, the Vikings ranged far and wide to find new places to trade or raid. They reached North America long before Columbus and even hauled boats over the mountains to trade and settle in parts of Russia. They are well known for their pioneering, adventurous spirit, so you will find people and places bearing elements of Old Norse names all over the world.

The Icelandic Sagas tell us how a man named Bjarni Herjolfsson was blown off course in AD 986 and sighted the coast of North America. He did not land but, about fifteen years later, Lief Eiriksson, son of Eirik the Red, did, some 500 years before Columbus. He called it Vinland, after the vines they found growing there. He and his men were principally searching for a supply of timber, a scarce commodity in Iceland and Greenland.

Vikings were unable to sustain a permanent colony there for more than about three years, due partly to fighting with the native Americans. In later centuries the saga claims were doubted, even though some of the native American tribes had a folklore of blond white visitors. A stone with runic inscriptions known as the Kensington Stone, supposedly unearthed in Minnesota has been discredited as a fake by weight of scientific opinion. However, remains of buildings including a smithy and a soapstone spinning whorl have been, generally, accepted as evidence of a Scandinavian settlement at L'Anse-aux-Meadows in Newfoundland. The remains of the buildings are similar to those of Icelandic dwellers from AD 1000.

Although the modern Norse Tradition shares many features with other Pagan paths (such as belief in a feminine divine as well as a male divine and a reverence for nature) there are many aspects that set it apart from Druidry, Wicca, etc. Some differences are superficial, such as giving the sun and moon, respectively, female and male polarity rather than the more common sun–male/moon–female of Wicca. Other differences are more far reaching, in particular the importance Odinists attach to oaths, reputation and keeping one's troth. These will be dealt with in detail in a later chapter, but suffice to say for the moment that these aspects form a very significant part of Heathen thinking. They have counterparts in some other traditions, but not to such a highly developed degree.

Incidentally, you may have noticed that I use the word Heathen instead of Pagan. Many Odinists prefer this term, although the two words have similar origins; the emperor-worshipping Romans dismissively called country dwellers (who still worshipped nature spirits) *Paganii*. 'Heathen' means a dweller of the heath, i.e. a person of rural habits, such as worshipping the old gods. (For an

3

overview of the range of Pagan paths, see *Paganism – a beginner's guide* by Teresa Moorey in this series.)

As with any religious path, some people are more committed or involved than others. To some people, simply toasting the Norse Gods occasionally is enough. Others join organisations, form groups (known as hearths), study the mythology, runes and magic or embark on environmental action. One has to decide upon one's own level of commitment and how far one's own circumstances, such as work, finance, home and family will enable you to get involved. Make no mistake, one can embark upon a fascinating, lifelong study. It can also be disruptive to one's relationships, attitudes to life and should, probably, carry a government health warning!

In exploring the path one will find many contradictions. Because hard archaeological evidence is difficult to find, with many texts fragmentary and enigmatic, people will inevitably put their own interpretations on the facts. Ultimately, there is disagreement and you must learn to sort facts from opinions. For example, you can read dozens of books about runes. Many authors will give the known facts about them, such as their names, shapes, sound and verses relating to them in old poetry. They will then go on to say that they have personally meditated on them and that, for them, the meaning of a certain rune is explained thus …. Of course, you can then find another author saying the opposite. Neither is necessarily wrong; the interpretation is right for each individual. You must decide which is right for you, or do your own meditation and come up with a third alternative!

I have tried to be as objective as possible in writing this book, but will inevitably be subjective in the opinions and personal prejudices I display along the way, so be aware that you must choose how much of it you accept.

There are also different versions of the myths, many of which disagree with each other. It is not surprising, as they developed by word of mouth between about AD 300 and AD 1200, in different languages, conditions and areas many miles apart. That situation isn't unique. The Christian Bible also has conflicting elements, such as the number of loaves and fishes varying between gospels. It is important to find the symbolic spiritual truth contained in such

4

stories, not the fiddly details. If you are interested in exploring this path it is essential, in order to find out what is true for you, to make comparisons between a range of texts. There is nobody around to say 'do it like this' or 'think like that' and that means you must determine ideas, actions and their consequences for yourself.

I believe that any worthwhile spiritual path should affect the follower's daily life, in both thoughts and actions. I also think that it should appeal to the intellect as well as the emotions and be relevant to the cultural roots and identity of the person involved. So before you immerse yourself in a new way of living, how about some practical work?

PRACTICE

1 Think about yourself. What do you know about your origins? Why not go to a library and find out the meaning and origin of your name? Do you feel you belong to the land and community in which you live? Do you feel you wish to have a closer affinity to the wildness of nature, or do you prefer to exercise your spirituality from the comfort of a warm room?

2 What do you want of a new spiritual path? What do you think are the advantages of the Norse Tradition for you personally and what would you gain from it? Conversely, what would the disadvantages be and what personal habits might you have to change to follow this path?

3 Do any of the place names in your locality have Old Norse or Saxon elements within them? The Saxons often used place-name endings such as 'ing' (people of), 'ton' (farm) and 'ham' (homestead), whilst the Danes often left their mark in place names finishing in 'fell', 'skaw', 'thwaite', 'by', 'beck', 'kirk' and 'gill'. Many of these names will be preceded by a personal name, for example, Nacton (called Nachetuna in 1086) in Suffolk, was originally made of the two elements *Hnakr* and *ton*, i.e. the farmstead of a man called Hnakr. Hnakr is a Norse-derived personal name and *ton* a Saxon word for a farmstead. Because it is situated in East Anglia, it could be assumed that this was originally a Danish settlement, since

the Danes provided the bulk of Norse influence in that area. However, there was nothing to stop a Saxon calling himself by a Danish name. Inevitably, spellings get changed considerably down the years.

Some English place names also contain the names of the old Gods. Look out for places with 'Grim' in the name, such as Grimsby or Grimsdyke. It is an *eke,* or nickname, of the god Woden or Odin in his hooded form. Thundersley in Essex is thought to have come from Thunorsley. Thunor is the Saxon form of Thor the thunder god, *leah* a Saxon term for a woodland clearing. There are also several 'Harrow hill' type names. It is believed that this denotes a traditional Saxon Pagan altar site, *hearg.*

Recommended reading

Gundarsson, Kveldulf, *Teutonic Religion*, Llwellyn, 1993

Harvey, G. and Hardman, C., *Paganism Today*, Thorsons, 1996

Herbert, Kathleen, *Looking for the Lost Gods of England*, Anglo Saxon, 1994

Hutton, Ronald, *Pagan Religions of the Ancient British Isles*, Oxford University Press, 1991

Jennings, Pete, *The Northern Tradition Information Pack*, The Pagan Federation, 1997

Jones, Prudence and Pennick, Nigel, *A History of Pagan Europe*, Routledge, 1995

Moorey, Teresa, *Paganism: a beginner's guide*, Hodder & Stoughton, 1996

Whitelock, Dorothy, *The Beginnings of English Society*, Pelican, 1997

BACK TO THE ROOTS

The origins of the Norse mythology and its associated beliefs and ideas are hard to pin down. What we do know is that there was an expansion of tribes out of the area we now know as Germany in the first few centuries AD. They were not a cohesive nation and different tribes found a variety of lands to conquer and occupy. It is said that the Saxons who originated from the Lower Elbe region were invited to England in AD 449 as mercenaries by Vortigern (the name translates as 'Overking'), in the period after the Romans had abandoned Britain, to repel attacks by Picts and Celts. Having achieved this, they decided to stay and overthrew their employer. In a decisive battle at Aylesford, Kent, in about AD 455 the Saxons were victorious under their leaders, the twin brothers Hengist and Horsa. Horsa died of wounds and was buried at the White Horse Stone, still visible today, and a sacred place to Odinists and others. Interestingly, Hengist translates as 'stallion' and Horsa as 'horse', so maybe they were ceremonial titles (like Vortigen) rather than their actual names. It was this band of Saxons who introduced a religion of Teutonic origins to England which differed from the Celtic and Roman beliefs which preceded them.

Other tribes went to what became known as Normandy (providing Britain with a further wave of conquerors in AD 1066). However, the bulk of the Germanic tribes occupied what we would now term Scandinavia – cold, often inhospitable lands with only narrow margins around the coast and fjords to sustain life through fishing and farming. Although we tend to think of them as warlike, most would have been more concerned with surviving through hard work on the land or sea.

The White Horse Stone, Kent

Their close proximity to the sea encouraged many to venture out far and wide as traders, with cargoes of fur and amber. As their wealth and families increased, there were no new lands for younger sons to inherit, as it was customary for the oldest son to inherit most. There was an important custom of uncles fostering each other's sons, to strengthen links between families and to provide a sort of boarding school between cousins. Bonds made in childhood, and hospitality received, would often mean that the recipients felt a lifelong bond of friendship or troth, very important when it came to defending each other.

They obviously put a great deal of thought into giving and receiving hospitality. There is a text called the Havamal (Sayings of the High One) which is a collection of homilies on how to live, the greater part of it concerned with hospitality. The Havamal forms part of a collection of Norse–Icelandic writings known as the *Poetic Edda*, written down in around 1270 but originating from much earlier. The

bulk of the thirty-five poems tell the mythology in verse form and are preserved in a manuscript called the Codex Regius which is held in Reykjavik, Iceland.

The other great literary source of knowledge also comes from Iceland, where many Scandinavians settled after disputes with authority at home. This second book is called the *Prose Edda* and was written by Snorri Sturluson in the early thirteenth century. Like the *Poetic Edda*, it was written in a society with Christian influences, but it contains the sources and details of many of the Norse myths we know today. It was written under the pretext of being a guide for poets on alliteration, form and *kenning*, possibly the only way such a text could be published at the time. Kenning, incidentally, is the art of finding other, more poetic, ways of saying things, for example, 'the sea' becomes 'the fishes' bath'.

The fact that Iceland is a major source of written information is perhaps significant. Iceland was one of the last countries in Northern Europe to be officially converted to Christianity, in about 1000. Even then, the law permitted individuals to sacrifice and worship the old Gods in the privacy of their own homes, as well as eating horseflesh (part of the staple diet for some Icelanders at that time but disapproved of by Christians). This gave the country a unique dual faith partly due, at least, from pressure from a significant part of the population. Within a few lifetimes, those rights were legally eroded, but Asatru was revived as an official state dual religion in 1973 due to the work of Sveinbjorn Beinteinsson and his friends. It means that today, a wedding conducted by a *gothi* or *gytha* (priest or priestess) of the old religion is recognised by the Icelandic authorities.

Women having rights to property, leadership and divorce, a legal system with a fixed table of damages for injury sustained and the village governed by a democratic assembly of freemen called a Thing, which gives origins to other parliaments such as the Tynwald in the Isle of Man. Does this sound like the barbaric races the monks wrote about? The Vikings did not do much writing, so we are left mainly with the heavily biased accounts of those they attacked. As the centres of wealth, monasteries were the obvious target for

9

Map showing a selection of migrations and invasions

KEY

■ VIKING SETTLEMENTS

↰ VIKING EXPANSION BY TRADE, RAID & EXPLORATION. WHERE ROUTES GO OVERLAND THEY SOMETIMES CARRIED BOATS UNTIL THEY REACHED A RIVER.

RUSSIA

SWEDEN

NORWAY

DENMARK
GERMANY

SHETLAND

ENGLAND

ICELAND

FAROES

ORKNEYS

GREENLAND

IRELAND

NORMANDY

NEW FOUNDLAND

those who came to raid instead of trade, as in 793 at Lindisfarne and elsewhere in the following two centuries. The Saxon, Celts and Picts all kept slaves, slaughtered prisoners of war and committed various other atrocities. The Viking raiders were no better or worse, but were written about in a more negative way. Incidentally, Viking refers to a mixed group of Scandinavian races who went raiding. To go a-viking was to go a-pirating and the warriors could be Danes, Jutes, Angles or any of the other tribes from that region. Saxon writers often called them all Danes.

Despite the bloodthirsty way in which they have subsequently been portrayed, the Norse peoples were very concerned with poetry and other fine things, such as jewellery and playing the board games *hnefatafl* and chess. It was thought (and still is by most modern Odinists) that one could achieve a measure of immortality by doing great things in one's life, which would then be put into a song by a *skald* (poet). The more spectacular the events, and thus the song, the longer it would be sung after one's death, providing a way of being remembered. In the early period of Norse beliefs, there was a fatalistic idea of one's life span being predetermined by the Norns, the three Wyrd sisters. One would not die until one's time was up, so warriors might as well live courageously and honourably. It is possible that belief in heavens such as the warriors' Asgard or the families Sessrunner Hall (under the protection of Freyja) did not come into consciousness until the later Viking and Saxon periods.

As they had beliefs about an afterlife and of a figure hanging on a tree wounded by a spear (Odin in his quest for the runes), those Norse and Saxons of Pagan beliefs must have been more easily converted to Christianity, although how genuine it was for people ordered to do so by their kings (sometimes at the point of a sword) is doubtful. Certainly, King Raedwald of East Anglia (buried at Sutton Hoo) accepted baptism from the King of Kent's priest as an act of political necessity, but set up the Christian altar alongside three heathen altars. His spectacular ship burial in about 625 was certainly a demonstrably Pagan affair. Perhaps if you already have several gods and goddesses, one extra doesn't seem important in that context. Although the Danes martyred King Edmund for his faith, in 869, for the most part they seemed content to let conquered peoples

continue with their original religion and frequently added it to their own, and in that sense they were more accepting of others' beliefs than Christianity was of theirs. Within a century of killing King Edmund the Danes were striking coins at his burial place (Bury St Edmunds) with his saintly image on them.

Olaf Tryggvasson, on the other hand, took a much less tolerant line. He was a Pagan when he won the Battle of Maldon in 991 (described in an old English poem of that name) and returned again with Svein Forkbeard in 994 to raid London and extract more Danegeld (ransom money). That winter, he stayed on at the Saxons' expense and was converted to Christianity. The following year when he began a five-year reign as King of Norway, he started a programme of very forced conversion which spread to its dominions such as Iceland.

The Norse did not leave much contemporary writing and, being mainly wooden, most of their buildings have disappeared. We do have a few reports about them from foreigners such as the Roman, Tacitus, who wrote about the Teutonic tribes' rune casting, and from the Saxons they attacked. What we are left with are some extensive burial sites. Norse leaders were often buried in mounds upon which stones with runic inscriptions were erected. In many places (such as Lindholm Hoje, Jutland, Denmark) the boat-shaped graves of less important folk are outlined in plain stones. The ship motif is obviously an important symbol to them. It features in their art and stories and the close proximity to the sea of their settlements meant that it was important for them to be successful sailors. They were not content to rely on similar ship designs to other groups, but developed the fastest, most efficient craft of their time. It is this adventurous spirit that shines through as the embodiment of their attitude – a forward looking, hardy and independent people. It is that same spirit by which the Norse tradition tries to live today – conscious of its great past history, but wanting to be accepted by the rest of the world on its own terms.

PRACTICE

1 Why not try to see some real Viking or Saxon artefacts for yourself? You could visit a local museum, or better still visit the Anglo Saxon section of the British Museum, Great Russell Street, London where treasures from Sutton Hoo and elsewhere are kept (Tel: +44 (0)171 636 1555). The Jorvik Centre Coppergate, York (Tel: +44 (0)1904 643211) is built over an archaeological excavation of the old Viking city and has some superb exhibits, including reconstructed scenes of the past complete with authentic sounds and smells! At the Vikingar Viking Heritage Centre, Barfields, Greenock Road, Largs, Scotland KA30 8QL there are films, tableaux and Viking God heads to be seen (Tel: +44 (0)1475 689777). You might like to visit the runic stones found in parts of Sweden, or the Viking Ship Museum in Oslo, Norway. There you can see both the Gokstad and Oseberg burial ships together with their associated grave goods, such as the Oseberg wagon.

2 The Norse mythology is too vast to even begin to give you a taste of it in a book such as this. I strongly advise you to get hold of a good authoritative version of some of the stories, such as the one by Crossley-Holland. You can read them at many levels – as exciting stories, as disguised histories or as the carriers of spiritual truths. It is good to compare more than one translation of the stories, to avoid being influenced by any individual author's opinions and interpretations. Beware though of Wagner's *Ring* Cycle opera! He took some mythological elements, added to them, changing and adding characters to make an epic work but it is a confusing menu of red herrings for the novice to swallow.

Recommended Reading

Anon, trans. Bill Griffiths, *The Battle of Maldon*, Anglo Saxon, 1994

Anon, trans. C. Larrington, *The Poetic Edda*, Oxford University Press, 1954

Barrett, Clive, *The Viking Gods*, Aquarian, 1989

Branston, Bryan, *Lost Gods of England, Gods and Heroes from Viking Mythology*, Book Club Associates, 1974

Campbell, James Graham, *The Viking World*, Windward, 1989

Care Evans, Angela, *The Sutton Hoo Ship Burial*, British Museum, 1989

Crossley-Holland, Kevin, *The Norse Myths*, Penguin, 1980; *Axe Age, Wolf Age*, Faber and Faber, 1985

Ellis Davidson, Hilda R., *Gods and myths of Northern Europe*, Pelican

Grant, John, *Viking Mythology*, Quintet, 1990

Jones, Gwyn, *A History of the Vikings*, Oxford University Press

Magnusson, Magnus, *Hammer of the North*, Book Club Associates, 1976; *The Viking Expansion Westwards, Iceland Saga*, 1973, *The Vikings*, 1980, all Bodley Head, *The Vinland Sagas*, Penguin, 1965

Stenton, Sir Frank, *Anglo Saxon England*, Clarendon, 1985

Stone, Alby, *Ymir's Flesh: North European Creation Mythologies*, Capall Bann, 1977

Sturluson, Snorri, trans. J. Young, *The Prose Edda*, University of California, 1954

Wilson, David, *The Vikings and their origins*, Thames and Hudson, 1972

3 BASIC BELIEFS

*H*istorically, the beliefs of the Norse and Saxon peoples varied greatly, both between different geographic areas, and at different times during the golden age of their first flowering, about AD 300 to AD 1000. A villager in fourth century Denmark may have had only three gods and goddesses. Because of poor communications, they may have been very different from the deities of a nearby village. Certainly, he wouldn't have known the whole range of stories which have been published today, although he might have known a few that we know have since been lost. Going back to that village a few centuries later, we might find entirely different deities being acknowledged, as ideas spread from elsewhere, or the needs of the community turned from protecting crops to ships. People tend to relate to the gods and goddesses they need and the same applies today.

One will find a huge variety of beliefs among followers of the tradition today. None of them are necessarily wrong, as they are each interpreting what is right and relevant within their own lives. Just as in the past, some will hold dear to one particular set of gods and goddesses. Some will be content in simple beliefs while others want to know the history and reasoning behind them. A few will be more involved than others and some will use their beliefs to work magic. Many will be content to just celebrate and acknowledge their faith either at each full moon or on specific festival days.

The Norse mythology has two families of deities, the Aesir and Vanir. There are well over a hundred known Norse deity names, excluding the multitude of *eke* names (nicknames) attached to some gods, as shown in the accompanying table. We do not know so

much about the Vanir, or as many of their names, but they appear to be an older family of nature gods, who, at some stage, battled with the incoming Aesir. Although some Aesir seem to have natural associations, such as Thor/Thunor with thunder, most seem to be more connected with civilisation, for example, his wife Sif's golden hair representing the golden corn of agriculture, which is cut off in mischief by Loki, who has to replace it with pure spun gold.

One should beware of seeing Gods by single attributes, as many are quite complex. For example, Thor/Thunor, one of the principal three Gods worshipped together with Odin and Frey is sometimes simply seen as a muscular guardian, hitting the *etin* (giant) enemies of Asgard. However, in one myth he engages a dwarf in a lengthy conversation to trick him into being there when the sun arises, which turns the dwarf to stone. This very different tactic shows a more intellectual side to our hero.

At the end of the war, hostages were exchanged, with the Vanir sea god Njord coming, with his son and daughter, Frey and Freyja, to live with the Aesir. Their names translate as Lord and Lady, the names with which many witches address their deities. It is interesting (and highly contentious) to speculate on that connection with them! Freyja is sometimes confused with Frigga, but they are very different characters. Whilst Frigga is associated with marriage and motherhood, Freyja takes many lovers. These include four dwarves, from whom she obtains the Brisingen necklace. No one can say for sure what the magical significance of the necklace was, but they are a feature of many goddesses over a long period in various parts of the world. It is said that as well as leading the Valkyries, who choose the best slain warriors for Valhalla, Freyja taught Odin, the chief Aesir God, the Vanir art of *seidr* magic, which was considered to be very different to the Aesir *galdr* magic.

He, in turn, taught it to others, but it was considered somehow unmanly. Odin has a huge range of attributes and names, connected with wind, war, masks, death, etc., but as the All Father God he is in constant pursuit of more knowledge and wisdom. He sacrifices one eye to gain it at Mimirs well, as well as hanging from Yggdrasil wounded by his own spear Gungnir to gain the runes. He has two

ravens, Hugin and Mugin (Thought and Memory), who survey the world for him and two wolves Freki and Geri (Greedyguts and Gobbler) who accompany him on some journeys. He also has a lightning-fast eight-legged horse called Sleipnir.

Odin had not always been the chief god, Tyr (or Tiw) appearing to have previously taken that role. Tyr takes a crucial role in the binding of the monstrous Fenris wolf, which is in danger of destroying the Gods if it cannot be subdued. A succession of cunning bonds is offered to it to test its strength, but it will not try the most effective without the surety of a hand placed in its mouth. Tyr is the only one courageous enough to do this, knowing that he will lose it when the Gods refuse to untie it again. Thus the one-handed God, Tyr, symbolises challenge, bravery and sacrifice.

Fenris was one of the terrible offspring of Loki, who also produced the Jormungand world serpent, Hel the guardian of the dead and Sleipnir, Odin's eight-legged horse. Loki starts as a trickster, often having to get the Gods out of scrapes which he has got them into. He gets more malevolent as tales develop, culminating in him causing the death of the pure sun-god Balder by means of a mistletoe dart. After some phophetic dreams, Balder's mother Frigga (wife of Odin, Goddess of housewives and fertility) had got all the plants to swear an oath not to harm him, but had missed out the mistletoe. The other Gods made a game of throwing missiles at Balder and watching them bounce off. Loki asks Hoder, Balder's blind brother, to join in after giving him the fateful dart and guiding him. For this act, and for showing no remorse afterwards, he is bound to a rock with a venom dripping snake above his head. His wife Sigyn undertakes to catch the poison in a bowl, shaking the world with earthquakes when she empties it. He is due to break free at Ragnarok, the final battle between the deities and forces of evil, which will be signalled by the blasts from a huge horn belonging to Heimdall, guardian of the Bifrost rainbow bridge.

It is stated in one text that the goddesses are equal in status to the gods, but unfortunately, there are far fewer individual stories about them. What we can tell from the stories is that, unlike many other mythological tales, they have minds and characters of their own,

independent of the male gods. This reflects the high position accorded to a woman in Norse society, where she was the keeper of the household and its keys and had property and divorce rights. This is also reflected in the Norse Tradition today, where men and women are seen as equals, with either having the ability to set up and govern a hearth group. In many other goddess orientated Pagan paths the woman is put in an ascendant position, such as witches, covens which are traditionally run by a High Priestess.

Many of the stories told about the gods and goddesses revolve around the constant threat to their world and family from the giants. Many of the giant names translate into terms for elemental natural forces, such as whirlpool, mountain, waterfall, etc. So it would seem that the gods are battling with nature itself. If you go back to the creation myths the early gods are often born of part-giant parentage. Thus they are fighting a war against part of themselves.

The tales take place around the nine worlds contained within the world ash tree Yggdrasil (meaning steed of the terrible one, Odin). Nigel Pennick suggests that Yggdrasil may be a yew. Yews were sometimes called 'needle ash' and it would make sense to have a tree that is evergreen, has a number of trunks and which exudes narcotic vapours. It would certainly provide a dangerous way to go on a shamanic journey, such as Odin's self-sacrifice, hanging for nine nights, wounded by his own spear to gain the secret of the runes. In the stories, various forces work for and against the continuity of the nine worlds, but eventually, Ragnarok, the final battle between good and evil is foretold, in which both sides are destroyed and a handful of survivors make a fresh start.

There are several ways in which we can regard the stories today. Firstly, as cracking adventure yarns. Secondly, as the carriers of esoteric knowledge or spiritual truths. Thirdly, we might perceive some of them as distorted or exaggerated versions of real historical events. I think there is an element of all these. The way we regard the stories is closely aligned to how we regard the gods and goddesses portrayed within them.

Table of Norse deities

All Aesir unless annotated V for Vanir. No pseudonyms used and the gender is not always constant. Names in small type in first three columns indicate non-deity i.e. Giant (Etin) human or dwarf.
Att. = Attendant of.

NB. It is always possible that some of the lesser names are *eke* names (nicknames) for deities featured elsewhere in the chart. Some deities such as Odin have many names or titles. The etymology of words is fraught with conjecture and debate and research is ongoing.

Name	Gender	Partner	Children	Attributes
AEGIR	m	RAN	9 Waves f	Sea
ALI	m			Marksman (also known as Vali)
ANNAR	m	NOTT	ERDA f	The other one
AUD	m			Prosperity
BALDER	m	NANNA	FORSETI m	Purity/light
BJORT	f			Beautiful
BLEIK	f			Blond one
BLID	f			Friendly one
BRAGI	m	IDUN		Poetry. Runes carved on tongue
BURI	m		BURR m	Producer
BURR	m	Bestla	ODIN m VILI m VE m	Son
BIL	f			Moment. Weaving
DAG	m	THORA		Day
DELLINGER	m	NOTT	DAG m	Dawn–third husband
EIRA	f			Medicine att. of Frigga
ERCE	f			Earth
ERDA	f			
FJORGYN	f		ODIN &THOR	Earth
FORSETI	m			Chairman Justice

Table of Norse deities (cont.)

Name	Gender	Partner	Children	Attributes
FREY (V) (or INGVI FREY)	m	Freygerda	Frodi m	Lord. Fertility Aesir Hostage
FREYJA (V)	f	OD ODIN Ottar Alfrigg Dvalin Berling Grerr	GERSEMI f HNOSS f	Lady. Sex, war. Frequently confused with Frigga. Last 4 dwarf lovers made Brisingen necklace
FRIGGA	f	ODIN	BALDER m	Fertility, house wives (MENGLAD)
FRITH	f			Pretty
FULLA	f			Full haired. Att. of FRIGGA
GEFION	f			Virgins. Att. of FRIGGA
GERSEMI	f			
GLENR	m	SOL		Opening in cloud
GNA	f			Att. of FRIGGA
HEIMDALL	m	Many lovers	3 Races	Guardian of Bifrost rainbow bridge
HEL	f	ULL		Guardian of Hel
HELGI	m	GUDRUN		
HERMOD	m			ODIN's messenger
HLER	m			Early sea God
HLIN	f			Consolation Att. of FRIGGA
HNOSS	f			Treasure
HODER	m			Blind son of Odin – killed Balder with Loki
HOENIR	m			Early God gave emotion and senses Bro. ODIN and LOKI

Table of Norse deities (cont.)

Name	Gender	Partner	Children	Attributes
HONIR	m			Indecisiveness
IDUN	f	BRAGI Ivuld		Spring. Immortal apples.
ING (V)	m			East Danes
IRPA	f			Dark Brown
KARI	m			Early God of Air
KVASIR (V)	m			Wisdom, mead
LODUR	m			Early God gave blood
LOFN	f			Eases path of true and illicit love
LOKI	m	SIGYN Thokk Angrboda	Sleipnir HEL f Fenrir Jormungland NARVI m VALI m	Lies, tricks evil, fire. After causing death of BALDER bound until Ragnarok
MAGNI	m			Might
MIMIR	m			His head is the oracle of a Well of Wisdom
MODI	m			Wrath
NAGLFARI	m	NOTT	AUD m	
NANNA	f	BALDER		
NARVI	m			Guts bind LOKI
NERTHUS (V)	f	NJORD	FREY m FREYJA f	Sea
NIGHT	f		NARVI m	Night
NJORD (V)	m	NERTHUS Skaldi	FREYJA f FREY m	Sea
NORNS;				Fates:
SKULD	f			Being
URD	f			Fate
VERDANDI	f			Necessity

The table of Norse deities (cont.)

Name	Gender	Partner	Children	Attributes
NOTT	f	NAGLFARI ANNAR DELLINGER	AUD m ERDA f DAG m	Night
OD	m	FREYJA	HNOSS f GERSEMI f	Left FREYJA
ODIN	m	FJORGYN FRIGGA RIND SAGA Grid	THOR m BALDER m HODER m TYR m BRAGI m HEIMDALL m ULL m VIDAR m HERMOD m VALI m SIGI m	Chief God – the Allfather. Runes and Wind. Many *eke* names. Ravens Hugin and Mugin (Thought/Memory) Wolves Freki and Geri. (Greedyguts and Gobbler) Spear Gugnir
OSTARA	f			Spring
RAN	f	AEGIR (wife/sister)	9 Wave maidens	Sea. Net to pull down sailors.
RIND	f	ODIN	VALI m	Frozen soil
SAGA	f	ODIN		Stories
SATAERE	m			Agriculture
SIF	f	THOR ODIN	ULL m	Golden corn hair ULL by ODIN
SIGI	m			Victor
SIGURD	m	BRUNHILD GUDRUN		
SIGYN	f	LOKI	NARVE m VALI m	Empties cup of poison
SKADI	f	NJORD ULLR	FREY m FREYJA f	Snowshoes
SKALDI	f	ODIN		Poetry
SKIRNIR	f			Shining one
SJOFN	f			Human passion
SNOTRA	f			Virtue. Att. of Frigga

The table of Norse deities (cont.)

Name	Gender	Partner	Children	Attributes
SOL	f	GLENR		Sun
SUMAR	m			Summer
SVASID	m		SUMAR m	Gentility
SYN	f			Trials, denial
THOR	m	SIF Iarnsaxa	MAGNI m MODI m	Thunder, law, Fertility. Has Hammer Mjollnir, Grid's belt and gauntlets of strength. His chariot is pulled by goats Tanngnost and Tanngrisni
TYR	m			War/ Courage. Chief before Odin. Lost hand to Fenris Wolf
ULLR	m	SKADI FRIGGA		Winter, archery.
VALI	m			Avenges Balder. Son of ODIN/RIND
VALI	m			Turned wolf to kill Narve (Son of LOKI)
VALKYRIES	f	– see list at end		Select slain for Valhalla
VARA	f			Beloved, Oaths.
VASUD	m		VINDSVAL m	Unfriendly
VE	m	FRIGGA		Early God – Brother of VILI
VIDAR	m			Will slay Fenris and survive Ragnarok
VILI	m	FRIGGA		Early God Brother of VE
VINDSVAL	m		WINTER m	Cold wind

The table of Norse deities (cont.)

Name	Gender	Partner	Children	Attributes
VJOFN	f			Conciliation Att. FRIGGA
VOR	f			Careful One Faith. Knowledge of future.
WINTER	m			Winter
WYRD	f		NORNS f	Early Goddess

VALKYRIES are led by Freyja in selecting the slain.

Name	Gender	Partner	Children	Attributes
ALVIT	f	Son of King Nidud		Allwise
BRUNHILD	f	SIGURD GUTTORM	Sigdrifa	Victory giver
GEIDRIFIL	f			Spear flinger
GEIRAHOD	f			Battle
GEIRAVOR	f			Spear goddess
GOLL	f			Screaming/fight
GONDUL	f			Magic animal
GUDRUN	f	HELGI SIGURD ATLI		
GUNN	f			Battle
GYNRITHIA	f			
HERFJOTUR	f			Army fetterer
HERYA	f			Devastate
HILDR	f			Battle
HJALMTHIMUL	f			Helmet clatterer
HLOKK	f			Shrieking
HRIST	f			Shaker
KARA	f			Stormy
MIST	f			Mist
NIPT	f			Sister
OLRUN	f	Son of King Nidud		Beer rune

The table of Norse deities (cont.)

Name	Gender	Partner	Children	Attributes
RADGRID	f			Bossy
RANDGRID	f			Shield destroyer
REGINLIEF	f			Daughter of Gods
ROTA	f			
RUSILA	f			Red haired
SANNGRINDR	f			Very violent
SHAKER	f			Mead bringer to ODIN
SIGRUN	f			
SKALMOLD	f			Sword time
SKEGGOLD	f			Battle axe
SKOGULL	f			Mead bringer to ODIN
SKULD	f			Blame
STICLA	f			
SVANHVIT	f	Son of King Nidud		Swanwhite
SVAVA	f			Put to sleep
SVEID	f			Noise
THOGN	f			Silence
THRIMA	f			Fight
THRUD	f			Power woman

There are also many dwarf and giant names recorded. Most of the giant names translate into uncomplimentary terms e.g. sooty face, hairy hands etc., but many others have meaning in various natural forces such as fire, snowdrift etc. Similarly, many of the place and river names translate into decriptions, e.g. Hel's underworld hall Eljuthnir means 'the one dampened by rain'.

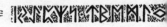

YGGDRASIL

THE WORLD ASH TREE - STEED OF ODIN. THOUGHT TO BE A 'NEEDLE ASH' I.E. A YEW TREE

ODIN AT HIGH THRONE OF HLIDSKIALF WITH HIS RAVENS HUGIN AND MUGIN PLUS WOLVE'S FREKI AND GERI. HIS EIGHT-LEGGED HORSE, SLEIPNIR, WAITS NEARBY

HRAESVELGR EAGLE WITH HAWK, VERFOLMR, SITTING BETWEEN EYES

RATATOSK SQUIRREL

HRIMFAXI, BEING DRIVEN BY NIGHT AND PULLING THE MOON MANI·CHASED BY WOLF HATI

YMIR'S SKULLCAP - THE SKY

SKINFAXI DRIVEN BY DAY AND THE SUN SOL BEING PULLED BY ARVAK AND ALSVID·ALL ARE CHASED BY WOLF SKOLL

COCK VIDFAIR

STAGS: DAIN, DUNEYR, DURATHÓR, DVALIN

YMIR'S BRAINS - THE CLOUDS

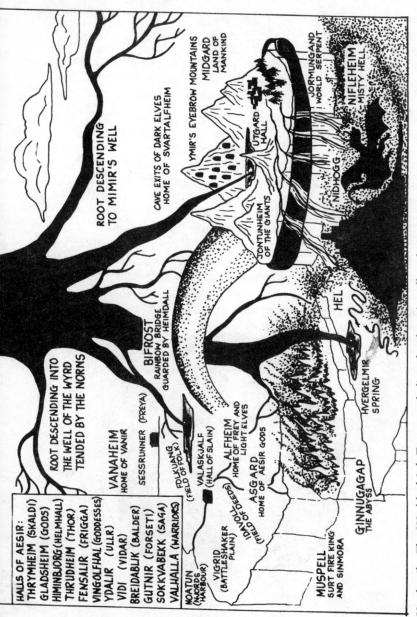

Yggdrasil – The World of Ash Tree, now believed to be a 'needle ash' i.e. yew

We can perceive the gods and goddesses as supernatural forces that have always been in existence. Alternatively, we could say that they are part of a group imagination and consciousness. For example, a tribe is worried about the success of its crops, so makes a goddess to protect them. By talking to her, acknowledging to each other she exists, she eventually does exist, for as long as people believe in her.

If that sounds far fetched, let's take a modern belief – the wind. Our Norse forefathers told of a giant eagle, Hraesvelgr, flapping his wings to cause the wind. Nowadays, meteorologists explain it by telling us about barometric pressure differences. The point is that, both then and now, we believe in a wind, without ever being able to see it. We can see its effects, such as leaves blowing along the ground, but until someone in the future comes up with another, more convincing, explanation people will have a belief in a phenomenon called the wind, just as they once had a belief in a flat earth. The belief in wind is one held in common with other people. Therefore, the wind exists. In the same way, a god or goddess created by a people will exist for as long as it is believed in, changing and taking on a life of its own as successive generations interpret it in slightly different ways.

Odin on Sleipnir

There is yet another option in how we regard our deities. Modern psychological thinking tells us how our minds are a collection of contradictory ideas. One part may say 'eat the chocolate, it is tasty.' Another says 'no, it is bad for you and will make you fat.' A third says 'who cares?' We can align our deities (or if you prefer, Jungian archetypes) as different personality traits and drives. Thus we might consider it is Loki, the mischievous god tempting us with the chocolate, Balder the Pure telling us to look after our body and Odin suggesting that we think independently. Going back to the idea about gods being of part giant parentage, one could think of the bar of chocolate as a giant, made of fat that is much like human or god fat! At a deep level, I think of my gods as aspects of my various personality traits, but on a daily basis it is easier to think of them as beings with individual characters and features, rather than some abstract psychological concept, and I speak as someone with four years of formal psychological training!

Many Odinists have a very direct and personal relationship with their gods and goddesses that does not need to be intellectualised and there is nothing wrong with a simple faith. That relationship tends to be very straightforward. The myths show us that the gods are more likely to admire a proud and independent spirit who acts honourably and doesn't make excuses for not achieving aims, than a sycophant who tries to suck up to them. They require respect, but not abject humility. In most cases in the myths, if they notice humans at all, they behave in a fairly arbitrary fashion towards them and are as likely to decide the outcome of a battle on the persuasion of a goddess lover rather than fervent sacrifice and prayer from below.

There is also another central set of ideas very important in understanding the beliefs of both the old and modern Northern Tradition. Many believe in a concept termed *wyrd*. This can be pictured as an infinite spider's web of threads, all connected to each other. Some of those threads are people's lives, which are controlled by the Norns or Wyrd sisters, who are Urd, Verdandi and Skuld, which translate as Fate, Necessity and Being. Thus, every action we take, trembles along the web and affects others. There is also an idea of *orlog*, which refers to a person's individual fate being fixed. Thus, one cannot change the date of one's death, but one can alter the way

in which it arrives. This belief may lead to a stoic attitude – if I am fated to die in battle today, I might as well do it bravely (and maybe get picked by the Valkyries to go to the warrior heaven Asgard) since I'm going to die anyway, whether I fight bravely or try to run away. There is historical evidence of Icelandic settlers letting the Gods of chance decide where they actually lived, by casting carved wooden high seat posts from their old home or temple overboard as they approached land. Where the seat posts beached was where they chose to live. This was done by Thorolfur Mostrarskeggi in 884 (in the Eyrbyggja Saga) and previously to that by Ingolfur Arnarson ten years earlier.

You will have read in Chapter 2 about how important family and tribal ties were. This is carried forward to today and true, Norse tradition, Pagans tend to be extremely loyal to their Hearth group, long after it has dispersed and seeded newer groupings. This especially applies to their original leaders. In this they parallel the loyalty expected of a man to his *eorlderman*, *gothi* or other leader in times past. It was considered a severe punishment for a leader to disown a member of his tribal group, because they would no longer have their lord's protection against theft, murder or slavery from outsiders.

There is a tradition of taking oaths on either a ring or sword (before the goddess of oaths, Vara) going back to those times. These oaths are taken extremely seriously and, in the Viking age, an oath breaker was often regarded as worse than a murderer. So Hearth members for example who has taken an oath to protect each other, regard that as an ongoing responsibility, regardless of what other circumstances or personal disputes might prevail. This feeling of mutual protection (whether done under oath or just by belonging to the same group) is known as 'Troth', and is a vital component of Norse tradition, which tends to set it apart from some other Pagan traditions.

Here is an example from my life of how 'Troth' works in practice.

A year or two ago, I was a guest with my wife at a large Pagan gathering which was taken over by half a dozen knife wielding neo-nazi thugs. We stood up to them and had our lives threatened. We both felt it was our duty to confront their desecration of the ritual, were aware that we were in danger but did not ask that anyone else put themselves on the line. We just suggested that people who

didn't approve left. From the far side of the circle of about a hundred people, a woman walked directly across and stood at my wife's other shoulder. I don't think the thugs had ever been confronted with two such formidably strong women before and eventually backed down. Aferwards, a friend said how brave, yet foolhardy the woman was. She replied that she had no choice in the matter. As a former member of our Hearth (disbanded when we moved away) she was still troth with us, despite a fairly major disagreement I had with her before the split. I think this is a good modern-day example of someone keeping their troth.

PRACTICE

1 What things might you want to consider before you take a personally binding oath?
2 The Norse Tradition uses magic to protect followers, which would seem from evidence to be successful. Aggressors can be repelled by magically directing all their hate back at them. Do you think that is ethically correct, or should followers leave fate (*wyrd*) to catch up with aggressors in its own good time?

RECOMMENDED READING

Anon, trans. G. A. Hight, *The Saga of Grettir the Strong*, Everyman, 1987

Anon, trans. Gwyn Jones, *Eirik the Red and other Icelandic Sagas*, Oxford University Press, 1988

Anon, trans. Palsson and Edwards, *Orkneyinga Saga*; *Egils Saga*, both Penguin, 1981

Anon, trans. John Porter, *Beowolf*, Text and translation, Anglo Saxon, 1991

Bates, Brian, *The Wisdom of the Wyrd*, Rider, 1996

Guerber, H.A., *Myths of the Norsemen*, Harrap, 1948

Harvey, G. and Hardman C., *Paganism Today*, Thorsons, 1996

Jesch, Judith, *Women in the Viking Age*, Boydell & Brewer, 1991

Magnusson and Palsom, *The Vinland Sagas*, Harmondsworth, 1965

Newton, Sam, *The Origins of Beowolf*, Boydell & Brewer, 1994

Sturlason, S. (ed. Monsen), *Heimskrugla*, Heffer, 1931

4

THE RUNES

R *unes are, at their simplest, marks scratched or written to convey an idea and yet the study of them can take place over the whole of one's life. This is such a vast and involved subject that I can provide only a basic introduction to it here. I have strong feelings about the runes and am concerned that they have been misused so often by so many people over the years. Let me start though, with their origins.*

Within the mythology, Odin hangs for nine days and nights from the world ash Yggdrasil, self-wounded by his own spear (*gugnir*), a sacrifice of himself to himself. At the end of the ordeal, he snatches the knowledge of the runes from the void, which I interpret as *Ginnugagap*. However it is looked upon, there is a clear spiritual message there – the runes require sacrifices of those who wish to know them and they are a serious pursuit, not some frivolous fortune-telling game. They are also firmly placed within Norse mythology and no others, so it would seem inappropriate for people following other religious paths to use them. After all, other mythologies have their own equivalents, such as the Celtic Druids' *ogham* script.

Historically, it is difficult to place the exact origins of the runes. For example, one character, *gyfu* is a simple diagonal cross. Just because someone carved a cross on to a rock in 300 BC doesn't mean that people were calling them, or using them as, a runic alphabet. In fact, strings of such symbols do not seem to have been associated together for at least another 600 years, in about AD 300.

There is some argument as to whether they grew up independently or were influenced by other alphabets. It is perfectly possible for two

people to invent similar simple marks without having seen the other's work. The early runes were made of straight lines, which is very important if you want to carve them into rock, wood or metal with crude tools. It was not until more sophisticated writing methods appeared that some of the forms became more rounded. It appears that the earliest alphabet of these runes had twenty-four characters. Just as the alphabet is made up of the first letters alpha and beta, runic alphabets are called *futhorks* or *futharks*, after the sound of their first six characters. From that Elder Futhark, as it is known, came many others, as the language and living conditions altered. For example, there is an Anglo Saxon futhork of only eighteen runes, but at the same time another one in Northumbria of thirty-two runes. There are other variations by geographic area (Iceland, Frisia, etc.) and by time period. The language and the way it was written developed over the 700 years that runes continued to be significantly used. In Scandinavian countries they frequently continued using runic script on gravestones when they had gone over to other methods for everything else. I sometimes wonder if it was more out of a sense of applying deliberately antiquated language for a sense of history, just as we might label a place 'Ye Olde Tea Shoppe.'

One has to remember that, in a mainly illiterate society, simple reading and writing would be regarded as magical in itself by those not trained in it, probably a large percentage of the population. The people who were educated, i.e. leaders and priesthood, would derive a certain amount of personal power just by being in on the secret. Within the myths, Bragi was given the power to speak with eloquence and poetry by having the runes carved on to his tongue.

It is clear that magical attributes were given to each rune. Some of these are evident from the rune poems that have survived from Iceland, Norway and England, where each verse details the properties of an individual rune. For example, *feoh* the first rune phonetically makes an 'f' sound, but each rune has an idea associated with it as well. In the case of feoh, this is cattle, which were a measure of someone's transferable wealth. In the table below you will see the associations for each of the twenty-four runes in the Elder Futhark.

The Elder Futhark of Runes

Names given to the runes vary considerably in form and spelling. Of the two given for each symbol, the first is more associated with Anglo Saxon language, the second with the Germanic languages.

Symbol	Sound	Names	Associations
ᚠ	f	feoh, fehu	Cattle, wealth, Frey
ᚢ	ur	ur, uruz	Aurochs, strength
ᚦ	th	thorn, thurisaz	Giant, obstacle, attack
ᚨ	a/o	os, as, ansuz	God, mouth
ᚱ	r	rad, raido	Wagon, travel
ᚲ	k	ken, kennaz	Torch, light, knowledge
ᚷ	g	gyfu, gebo	Gift, sex
ᚹ	w/v	wyn, wunjo	Joy, good news
ᚺ	h	hagel, hagalaz	Hail, bad weather, air
ᚾ	n	nid, naudiz	Need, distress
ᛁ	i	isa, isaz	Ice, stasis
ᛃ	j/y	gera, jeraz	Harvest, year, fruitful
ᛇ	eo	eoh, yr, ihwaz	Yew, bow, earth
ᛈ	p	peorth, perthro	Unknown, birth, dicecup
ᛉ	e	elhaz, algiz	Protection, elk
ᛊ	s	sigil, sowilo	Sun, heat
ᛏ	t	tyr, tiwaz	Tyr, courage, battle
ᛒ	b	beorth, berkanan	Birch, healing, woman
ᛖ	eh	ehwho, ehwaz	Horses, adventure
ᛗ	m	man, mannaz	Man, Mankind
ᛚ	l	laguz, laukaz	Leek, water
ᛜ	ing	ing, ingwaz	The God Ing
ᛟ	o	odal, othala	Home, land, tribe
ᛞ	d	Daeg, dagaz	Day, balance

You can obtain many books on runes and most will contain extended meanings and associations for each character. They are all valid to the individual authors, but are not all based on hard historical fact. For that reason, I have chosen not to add to the many conflicting ideas and have only given the basic details. *Runes for beginners* by Kristyna Arcarti is another book in this series that you may wish to study further, plus those in the reading list at the end of this chapter.

You can use runes in several ways and writing is, obviously, the primary one. Our ancestors were very fond of inscribing their possessions with names, etc. Sometimes they wrote out the whole futhark, maybe thinking that their magic would cover every eventuality! When you write in runes, it is most usual to write phonetically, that is, how words sound, not how they appear in modern English (or any other language written in Roman letters). So, for example, if you wanted to write the word 'fearing' you would just use feoh, *isa*, *rad* and *ing*. You can also use some runes as a sort of shorthand, when they stand for a generally recognised idea. For example, you could simply use the feoh rune instead of writing out the word 'cattle'.

The Roman writer Tacitus describes the Teutonic tribes as marking slivers of fruiting tree wood and casting them on to a white cloth to make a divination before any important decision was taken. Some of us still do that today. Methods vary, but many depend on a three-rune system, in which the first represents the person and their question, the second the possible answer and the third the eventual consequences leading on from the situation. One can devise all sorts of more complicated systems, none of which will have historic origins but will be effective if you use them consistently, confidently and they mean something to you.

This personal relationship with runes is something you can build up only by repeated study and meditation. They are a hard and demanding master or mistress, but rewarding with it. When you have a firm idea of what a rune means to you, you can use it in magic. You can chant it, inscribe it on a talisman or make the shape of it in the air with a staff, wand or finger. You can even put your own body into runic postures and more than one person has tried to develop a form of 'runic yoga'.

One way in which runes can be used very powerfully is to combine several into what is known as a *sigil* or *bindrune*. You should be careful when doing this though, as it is very easy to create a third, unwanted rune by combining two others, as I show in the following figure.

Bindrune

The runic futhark is usually divided into three *aetts*. The first third is Freyjas Aett, the second Hagels Aett and the last Tyrs Aett (see figure below). Historically, the runes always seem to have followed the same order, with the occasional exception of the last two, *odal* and *daeg*, which have sometimes switched places.

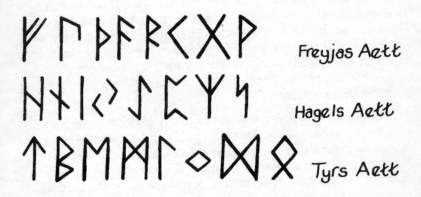

The Elder Futhark

You might not want others to read and decipher what your intentions are, so bindrunes can be quite useful in this. The other way is to use a code. In the following figure I have given examples of codes from history. If you used these, others could read the same sources and decipher them, so you are advised to devise your own. Each example uses a two-part code. The first number indicated refers to the aett (or family of eight if you prefer to think of it that way) in which the rune occurs. The second number indicates that particular rune's order within that aett.

Whisker and Tent runes

pRactice

1 Now try coding some runes for yourself. Start by writing gyfu as a 'whisker' code. Then write *tyr* and *ken* in the form of a 'tent rune'.
2 Write your own name in runes. Do not forget to spell it how it sounds, rather than how it is spelt in Roman characters. That means double letters are written only once (such as the double 'n' in my name, Jennings) and that some names may appear shorter due to a rune making the sound of several letters. For example, a single thorn rune substitutes the sound by the letters 'th'.

3 Read the figure below. What does it say?

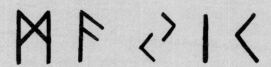

Runic inscription

4 Why not make your own set of runes? It is far better both
magically and cheaper than buying them. Choose a tree
branch about 3 cm (1.5 inches) in diameter of a variety that
bears fruit or nuts. If you cannot find a good naturally fallen
branch, ask the tree's permission (and the owner's!) before you
cut it and leave a gift in return. Dry it out naturally and saw it
into slices. You will need at least twenty-four for the Elder
Futhark, including a few spares in case of mistakes in carving.
Then carve the shape of a rune on to each, meditating on its
meaning and shape as you do so. (You might like to spread
this exercise over a long time period.) When they are carved,
colour the indentations red. Some people add a few drops of
their own blood to the paint to bond them personally to the
runes. Finally, varnish them and make a drawstring bag to
keep them safely together. Incidentally, some people make a
blank 'wyrd' rune as part of a set, to represent the unknown. I
have yet to see any convincing historical evidence for the
existence of such an idea and regard the *peorth* rune as
serving this purpose.

5 Try and read several people's interpretations of the runes.
Inevitably, many books draw upon the limited archeological
artefacts available as a source of knowledge. Make sure you
read translations of the old rune poems, which are reproduced
in several of the books listed below.

Recommended Reading

Arcarti, Kristyna, *Runes for beginners*, Hodder & Stoughton, 1994

Fries, Jan, *Helrunar*, a manual for rune magick, Mandrake, 1993

Howard, Michael, *Mysteries of the Runes*, Capall Bann, 1994

Kemble, J.M., *Anglo Saxon Runes*, 1840 reprint, Anglo Saxon, 1991

King, Bernard, *The Elements of the Runes*, Element, 1993

Linsell, Tony, *Anglo Saxon Runes*, Book and cards, Anglo Saxon, 1992

Morgan, Keith, *Rune Magick*, Pentacle Enterprises, 1993

Osborn and Longland, *Rune Games*, Penguin

Page, R.I., *Reading the past: Runes*, British Museum, 1991

Pennick, Nigel, *The Secret Lore of Runes and other Ancient Alphabets*, Rider, 1991

Peschel, Lisa, *A Practical Guide to the Runes*, Llewelyn

Peterson, Dr. James M., *The Enchanted Alphabet*, Aquarian, 1988

Pollington, Stephen, *Rudiments of Runelore*, Anglo Saxon, 1995

Thorsson, Edred, *At the Well of the Wyrd: A handbook of Runic Divination*, 1990; Weiser, 1987

5

CLUES FROM
FOLKLORE

*F*olk customs frequently preserve knowledge that would otherwise be
lost, because oral traditions have been marginalised for centuries
by academics. They frequently find it hard to accept that a truth can
survive (albeit in a sometimes distorted form) without the benefit of
someone writing about it. This still happens today, despite the fact that
historians do often find elements of truth independently that are then
confirmed by the traditions they have previously ignored.

Before we can use folk traditions as a tool for learning about
heathen beliefs, we need to have a firm idea of what constitutes a
folk tradition. Folklorists may argue about this all night (and
frequently do!) so to simplify matters I will give you my definition:
a song, dance or custom that has been carried on, mainly by being
handed down orally from one person to another, for 100 years or
more. It should have survived without the interference of authority
(such as school, Church) in its performance, which is principally
carried on because the people involved want it to.

That might sound a bit long winded, but it means that people carry
customs on purely because they want to and that the custom still
has some meaning for them. Inevitably, this will mean that the
custom may well change over the years to accommodate changing
social conditions or attitudes. It also means that folk customs
should not become fossilised museum pieces – they must remain
alive and adaptable to mean something to the participants. When
they fail to have meaning, the custom will be dropped, or carry on
only as a confused, archaic parody of itself.

Carrying on those traditions is an important responsibility and in Viking society, a *skald* i.e. a poet who wrote, declaimed and sang about the historic events of his community, was regarded with awe as the living history book of the tribal group. A leader is not great unless someone else says so and maybe that's why skalds were held in very high regard. It is evident also that the tribal leaders themselves were expected to have a grasp of poetry, as well as being able to fight and to speak the law.

Of course, we have nearly lost many traditions through changes in society. In England, Cromwell's Puritans suppressed a large number of customs in the 1600s and the police have called a halt to many more over the years that were perceived as too drunken and rowdy. The invention of the record player and radio stifled many traditional singers, ashamed at what were now thought of as old-fashioned country yokel songs. Yet, whenever the end seems nigh, the strength of some of the songs, dances and customs succeeds in winning a new generation of enthusiasts. We also continue to invent and discard many new customs. In recent years there has been a trend towards laying flowers at the spot where a person has died, rather than on their grave and the imported custom of extravagant street carnival has established itself firmly in Notting Hill, London, as an exuberant event larger than the carnival in Rio de Janeiro.

Many English speaking people have little awareness of the rich variety and depth of our folklore. There are thousands of traditional songs, dances, stories and customs often happening under the noses of people who do not appreciate what we possess. Not every bit of folklore contains Pagan belief and the bad research of ill-informed writers who have labelled everything as Pagan fertility customs has a lot to answer for. In his valuable book *The Stations of the Sun*, Professor Ronald Hutton explodes some of those myths by showing that many traditions did not start until medieval times, hardly a heyday of rampant Paganism. He also attacks the theories presented in Frazer's monumental collection of traditions from around the world, *The Golden Bough*, which has held sway with academics for the best part of the twentieth century. The details of the many native religious practices he researched are good, but suggesting that they

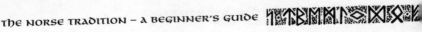

all have a connection to one particular belief and priesthood is patently absurd. However, *The Golden Bough* remains a valuable source of raw data if one takes its conclusions with a large sprinkling of salt.

Do not let these arguments put you off exploring the rich European folk heritage, but be aware of the pitfalls. Professor Hutton's apparent distrust of anything that hasn't got a written record can be as restricting to the truth as believing everything you are told. Remember that most customs are, today, ignored by those who write. A few centuries ago, when the upper classes often kept a greater distance from the quaint practices of the peasantry this was even more the case. I have enquired at Tourist Board offices, town halls, newspapers and libraries about customs currently happening in their own district, to be confronted by complete ignorance. I have gone into churches and pointed out 'green man' carvings that do not appear either in the official church guide or the mind of the priest.

There is an exciting world out there waiting to be explored by the enthusiastic and open-minded Pagan. Not all of the folklore I am about to detail is strictly of the Norse or Anglo Saxon traditions, but it is native to Northern Europe and, in most cases, it is impossible to be certain of the origins of traditions because they are so old. By looking and listening, we can get a feel for the beliefs of our ancestors. There is no substitute for actually experiencing a folk event, be it finding a Pagan carving, watching morris dancers or listening to a traditional singer. Looking at photographs and listening to recorded music does not convey the same sense of occasion and atmosphere. All the time you are experiencing these things, try to think what is going on beneath the surface of jollity and drinking. What is the meaning of that bizarre man/woman sweeping the way clear for the dancers? Would a magical view clarify the storyline of the song being sung? Could the movements of the dance be used as a way of raising energy in a ritual? Would the music, exhaustion, dizziness and working in unity with other people provide a way of reaching an altered state of consciousness?

SACRED SITES

Most stone circles and monoliths have their origins in prehistory, but a large percentage have continued to be used for Pagan rituals throughout the centuries. In many old churches, carvings that have little to do with Christianity and far more to do with natural deities can be found. They can be inside or outside, obvious or obscure. Look out for the 'green man', with foliage issuing from his mouth, or the woodwose with striped bare skin and a club. In some areas the sheila-na-gig can be found, a female figure displaying her vulva, whilst elsewhere tongue-pokers of either sex can be found in stone carvings, wooden bench ends or as gargoyles. Dragons and other mythical beasts are often shown being defeated by saints. You can sometimes find the figure of a man with a lion, calf and eagle. These are the symbols of Matthew, Mark, Luke and John of the Christian gospels, showing how they once borrowed heavily from the earlier Heathen imagery that they tried to supplant.

The Green Man

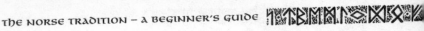

Dance and Ritual Drama

Best known of English traditions is the morris dance. Whether it had Pagan origins or not is hard to say, but it certainly feels that way now. There are several different variants: the Cotswold Tradition is the best known, as a collection of dances from villages in the Cotswold area of Oxfordshire. The dancers wear white clothes, with bells on their legs and they carry handkerchiefs or sticks. Some morris dancers claim it is a 'males only' dance, but there is historical evidence to the contrary, such as the woman who accompanied Will Kemp on a marathon dance in the mid-1600s. Today you can see men's, women's and mixed sides of six dancers each. The dancers of the North West Tradition (from the North West of England) wear clogs, and progress along in their dances, rather than staying in one spot. The Border Morris of the Welsh Borders wear clogs, but also black their faces. In East Anglia and Kent the Molly Dance has been revived, in which the dancers wear farm labourers' clothes or suits of tatters, and often black their faces in ritual disguise. Most areas have sides who dance traditions other than their own. Some morris sides are associated with other folk spectacles, such as providing mummers' plays, which are traditional, ritualised death and resurrection plays with magic and laughter in them. Ritual sword dancers also frequently re-enact ritual murder as they lock swords around their captain's throat in mock decapitation. Of course, you do not have to belong to a dance side to experience English folk dance. In recent years there has been a revival in interest in barn dances and *ceilidhs*. The usual pattern is for everyone to be walked through the dance first, so even complete beginners can have a great night's fun, to the sound of traditional folk music.

Other specific events happen at different times of the year. Below are some that happen in Britain, but you will, no doubt, find local variations around the world. From historical example it seems that Vikings were always keen to take on the folk beliefs and customs of the lands they migrated to and this gives us a good example to live by now. We all have a need to celebrate communally in life and it is a part of human nature to identify with one's ancestral roots.

The Shetland Islanders of Lerwick revived interest in their Viking roots by 'inventing' a ship-burning celebration known as Up Helly Aa about 100 years ago. It still survives and has become an annual tradition on the last Tuesday in January, because people want it to and are still proud to identify with their Scandinavian ancestors.

The Oss at Padstow, the Abbots Bromley Horn Dance, the Burning Barrels at Ottery St Mary and the Haxey Hood Game are just a few of the many annual seasonal festivals. In most parts of England there are customs relating to beating the bounds of a parish, administering a charity or quit rent, conducting a mock trial or election, etc. Some have continuous histories going back many hundreds of years, whilst some have been rediscovered and revived. You can locate many of them from the recommended reading list at the end of this chapter.

Abbots Bromley Horn Dance

I am proud to take part in two events in my native area of Britain, East Anglia, and would urge all Heathens to support or join in whatever is appropriate in their own area. Each year, my Hearth makes a 'Jack of the Green' figure for me to wear, from branches of greenery, which we bring to life in a ritual on the eve of Mayday (1 May). On Mayday morning, we arise to greet the sunrise over the sea at Felixstowe (at around 5:15 a.m.) with the East Suffolk Morris Men and I wear the suit of leaves, which completely covers me. The Morris Men always like to have the Jack of the Green present when they dance up the Mayday sun, just like many of the other dance sides who make the effort that morning.

On 26 December I can be found at Middleton, Suffolk, as part of a Cutty Wren ceremony. Years ago I read that it was the only place in England that had such a tradition, but it had died out around the turn of the century. Chatting to some dancers and musicians in a session one night, the idea was born to revive the event. We formed a molly dance team called Old Glory and we have a torchlit procession, led with a carved wooden wren, dancing and music. Each year I sing the traditional songs and retell the story of how the wren became the king of the birds. There must be many such customs waiting for the right people to revive them. It certainly means something to the people taking part or watching, as more than 100 turn out each year for it. You will notice that in reviving the tradition we have used a carved wren, not a killed wren. This is just one of the ways in which traditions adapt to changes in public attitude.

folksong and music

Few British folksongs are explicit about magic and the supernatural, but it is sometimes possible to gain a magical understanding of them from some small clue. There were times when it was dangerous to sing about such things anyway. One must also remember that the bulk of the British repertoire today was saved by collectors at the

turn of the twentieth century, who fearing that many would die out due to industrialisation and mass entertainment, travelled around Britain and America collecting the songs. Many of those collectors were Christian vicars, whose informants were often shy about revealing some of their bawdier material to such men. One must remember this was the end of the Victorian age, with a hypocritical and prudish attitude to anything regarded as un-Christian. If a collector did manage to take down a risqué ballad, he or she could never publish it as such.

If you hear a line in a song referring to 'A Gay Green Gown' it often refers to a witch or magician. There is one song called just that from the New Forest in the south of England, together with some others contained in an out-of-print book by Ruth Tongue called *The Chime Child*. In 'The Broomfield Wager', recorded by several people including the man from whom I learnt it, Cyril Poacher, the broom is an ingredient to a magic sleeping draught. The woman outwits the man, returning from a field with her virginity intact, despite his assistant's magic actions. Without that explanation, the song makes little sense. There is a similar but more obvious theme of a male magician trying to bed a female magician in 'The Two Magicians', recorded by, amongst others, the group Steeleye Span. This group has made some splendid recordings of many other magical songs as well, including 'Thomas the Rhymer' and 'Tam Lin', which are both songs about people seized by the faery folk. Also in Steeleye Span's repertoire are versions of three ritualistic murder songs, 'Little Sir Hugh', 'Outlandish Knight' and 'Long Lankin'. Other songs to listen out for are the various Cutty Wren songs, seasonal songs for maying, etc., 'John Barleycorn' and two about mythical beasts exaggerated to monstrous proportions, 'Derby Ram' and 'Lambton Worm'. If you ever come across a Scottish song called 'Nicky Tans' (about the string some people tie around the bottom of their trouser legs) it has a single line in it referring to 'the horseman's grip and word', the only time I have detected a mention of horse whisperers' magic.

pRACTICE

1 Try to find some interesting carvings of the types I have mentioned.
2 Try to visit an ancient sacred site, such as a stone circle or standing stone. Take your time and be quiet and respectful around it. Place your hands on the rock and see if you can feel a vibration from it. Take a compass and check how the site is aligned. Does the compass behave erratically when near the stones?
3 Go and see some traditional singing, dancing or custom and join in, if possible. Can you use anything you experienced within a ritual setting?
4 Research the folklore of the area in which you live. Is there any event worth reviving or one in decay that could do with a fresh injection of life? The English Folk Dance and Song Society (EFDSS) has a research library, the address of which is given below.

Recommended reading

Anderson and Hicks, *The Green Man*, Harper Collins, 1990
Child, Frances, *The English and Scottish Popular Ballads*, Houghton Mifflin, 1965
Frazer, Sir James, *The Golden Bough*, Papermac, 1987
Green, Marion, *A Harvest of Festivals*, Longman, 1980
Hole, Christina, *A Dictionary of Folk Customs*, Paladin, 1986
Howard, Michael, *The Sacred Ring*, Capall Bann, 1995
Hutton, Prof. Ronald, *The Stations of the Sun*, Oxford University Press, 1996
Oxford Book of Ballads, Oxford University Press, 1989
Palmer, Roy, *Everyman's Book of English Country Songs*, Dent, 1979
Pennick, Nigel, *Crossing the Borderlines: Guising, Masking and Ritual Animal Disguises in the European Tradition*, Capall Bann, 1997
Shuel, Brian, *National Trust Guide to Traditional Customs of Britain*, National Trust, 1986

Stewart, Bob, *Where is St. George? Pagan imagery in English folksong*, Moonraker Press, 1977

Williams and Lloyd, *Penguin Book of English Folk Songs*, Penguin, 1980

English Dance and Song magazine and *The Folk Directory* available from the English Folk Dance and Song Society, Cecil Sharp House, 2 Regents Park Road, London, NW1 7AY, UK

Recommended Listening

There is no substitute for seeing and hearing folk traditions in live performance but, if that is impossible, listen to:

Fairport Convention – *Liege and Lief* (Chrysalis CDP 3214672): includes 'Tam Lin'.

Steeleye Span – *Best of Steeleye Span* (Chrysalis CDP 321487–2): includes 'Little Sir Hugh', 'Long Lankin', 'Demon Lover', 'Elf Call', 'Thomas the Rhymer'.

Steeleye Span – *Time* (Park PRKCD34): includes 'Cutty Wren', 'The Elf Night' plus two contemporary Pagan songs.

Various – *English Customs and Traditions* (Saydisc CD-SDL 425): includes Padstow, Helston, Castleton, Abbots Bromley, Mummers, etc.

The Watersons – *Frost and Fire* (Topic): ritual songs.

6

LIVING WITH THE NORSE TRADITION TODAY

The Norse Tradition is not a glorified re-enactment society, of people dressing up in costume and imitating their ancestors. It promotes the spirit of their age, rather than the actuality. In any case, the much vaunted rape, pillage and plunder would be rather frowned upon nowadays! The Vikings were very modern, forward-looking people for their time, using the best of available technology. They also had a specific mythology and religion we can still relate to, even if we cannot emulate the way they carried it out. For example, like many religions of the past they did sacrifice humans, certainly at the temple at Uppsala, Sweden and probably at the grave mounds of important people (as the Anglo Saxons did at the Sutton Hoo, England, burials).

Unless you are willing to study Old Norse or Old English you are not going to be able to conduct rituals in that same language. Some people do just that and provide a translation for others but, of course, although they can write rituals in the language, few words of ritual have survived from those times. So, as modern Odinists we are faced with the task of reconstructing rituals, or developing new ones, using whatever clues we can find in written texts, pictures and folklore. We can use details we know from the mythology (e.g. the hammer used in blessing a wedding), as a focus for the modern words and actions we put together.

It is no good, though, constructing rituals for gatherings, unless they are allowed to have a practical effect on your daily life. You can live the faith in many ways, dependent on your capabilities and situation. I changed career, as a result of my Heathen beliefs, from sales to counselling, which I saw as being more related to my

spiritual path. You may choose to mix with a particular circle of friends who are sympathetic to your beliefs, or to get involved in helping the survival of our physical environment. Some of the ways in which you react on a daily basis may be dictated by the particular path you choose within the tradition. Someone aspiring to be a *gothi* (priest or priestess) must have regular contact with other people, whilst a more shamanic role, such as *volva*, would demand that its practitioner spend a lot of time close to nature, in the countryside.

There is also a sense of how one faces adversity as an individual within the Norse Tradition. The examples from the past show us that Odinists would stay true to their word and tribe, whatever the personal cost, often with a stoic or fatalistic view of life based on the concept of the web of the *wyrd*. A promise is seen as a sacred thing, so Odinists do not give them lightly.

Generosity is a much vaunted attribute in many Saxon and Norse texts, especially 'ring giving', in which a faithful warrior or servant is rewarded with arm or finger rings, a form of currency. He can choose to pass part of that honour on to his wife or children who may have assisted him in some way. Thus, honour is publicly spread and the bond between the giver and receiver strengthened.

One must also live as closely as possible to the Havamal and, as that is largely concerned with hospitality, one must seek to be both a generous and welcoming host and a valued guest. It is the custom in many of our families for the woman of the house to offer mead to visitors on arrival. (Mead bearers are traditionally women, but of course today, there is no reason why the honour cannot be shared.) On a practical note, have you considered brewing your own mead, wine or beer? There is a great emphasis on practical skills within Norse Tradition and this one combines the satisfaction of being independent and thrifty with enjoyment and personally providing a part of the feast that accompanies each ritual or guest welcoming.

We must study our chosen path well and not be afraid to defend it against all comers. Our directness can be seen as confrontational to others (including, at times, the wider Pagan community) but is a result of trying to live open, honest lives, respecting the role of women and nature and striving to maintain a good reputation. Odinists should be

A mead horn

ethical and should uphold the law. In fact, in ancient Iceland, each gothi priest was also a law speaker, i.e. the two activities were intertwined. It makes for some hard choices regarding one's personal standards and where to draw the line. No one else can tell you what to do. As a member of the Norse Tradition you should be independent and free thinking, capable of deciding your own answers.

PRACTICE

1 What would you do if you were confronted by an intruder in your house, who was threatening your family, and why?
2 Find an environmental activity with which you can get involved. It could be recycling your household waste, nature conservation work or forming part of a protest action against something that threatens the natural environment.
3 How open can you be about your beliefs? Some people will have natural difficulties in 'coming out' to their family, friends or work colleagues. Consider how you can best deal with this, in a way that informs without trying to proselytise. Is it wiser to leave some people in ignorance, or will it cause continuing tension as they make false assumptions about your beliefs?

4 How about having a go at some home brewing. There are plenty of books available on how to make wine and beer, but I have included one in the list below that will enable you to make the ritual honey drink of Norse mythology, mead.

RECOMMENDED READING

Aswynn, Freyja, *Leaves of Yggdrasil*, Llewellyn, 1990

Beswick, Francis, *Traditional British Honey Drinks*, Heart of Albion Press, 1994

Dimmbla, Gothrun, *Odsmal*, Freyjukkettir, 1996

Flowers, Stephen (who also writes as Edred Thorsson), *The Galdabrok: An Icelandic Grimoire*, Weiser, 1989; *Fire and Ice*, Llewellyn, 1990

Hollander, Lee M., *The Saga of the Jomsvikings*, University of Texas, 1990

Pagan Dawn magazine, The Pagan Federation, BM Box 7097, London, WC1N 3XX, UK

Pennick, Nigel, *Practical Magic in the Northern Tradition*, Thoth, 1989

Stone, Alby, *The Well of Ymir*, Heart of Albion Press

7

IT'S MAGIC!

SEIÐR MAGIC

*I*n the Saga of King Hrolf *we get a few glimpses of some powerful magic at work. Queen Skuld chants incantations to defeat opposing warriors and from the magic she weaves, from a scaffold erected in a black tent, a monstrous boar appears, shooting arrows from its bristles. One wonders if this is the magic of* fylga *i.e. projecting one's spirit into a remote situation as a fetch. Certainly some sectors of the Asatru tradition believe in a guardian spirit called a* hamingja, *which can attack or be attacked.*

A more gentle kind of magic is at work in the *Saga of Eirik the Red* when a visiting volva called Thorbjorg, the Little Sibyl, is welcomed at Brattahlid, Iceland. She arrived wearing a blue cloak with jewelled straps right down to the hem, a black lambskin hood lined with white catskin, glass beads about her neck and a staff topped with a brass knob and set with stones. She wore a touchwood belt from which hung a skin bag for her charms. Hairy calfskin shoes and catskin gloves completed the outfit. She was honoured with the best of food, and given a high seat, with a hen feather cushion, to survey the assembled throng. She asked for assistance from the women in chanting a spell called Varthlokur, or Spiritlocks, but only one, a Christianised woman called Gudrid was able to, after some reluctance. The text goes on to say all the women gathered in a circle around the platform on which Thorbjorg was seated and the chant was eventually recited by Gudrid, after which prophecy was given. Both these examples would seem to fit into what we would

term *seidr*, that intuitive, and largely feminine-based, magic of the Norse Tradition.

Note that there is both the positive and negative at work here. The sagas do not contain any equivalent of the wiccan 'An it harm none' ethic. That is not to say that one should not be applied now, as an ethical way of working. I am a firm believer that there is a cost for all magic performed, good or bad, and that evil will bring its own reward. Although there may not be specific texts telling you not to work magic for negative ends, there are plenty that will tell you that your good reputation and the way you face adversity are very important.

Such considerations obviously never bothered the mother Helga and aunt Frakokk of Harold Hakonarson (Smooth Tongue), Earl of Orkney, in the *Saga of Orkneyinga*. They prepared a white linen shirt, threaded with gold, for his brother Paul. When Harold put it on instead, his flesh started to quiver and he died in agony, in place of his brother. In that same saga, the mother of Sigurd helps her son overcome being outnumbered seven to one in battle by means of a magical raven banner she weaves. It has the property of ensuring victory, but at the cost of each of its bearers being killed in the battles.

Galdr magic

Men work their magic too in the sagas, but in different ways, often by use of the runes. In *The Saga of Egil* the hero corrects the badly written runes of another that are causing a sick girl to get worse rather than better. One can take that as a lesson to us all in being careful in our choice and inscription of runes. In the *Saga of the Jomsvikings* both King Gorm and Earl Harold pay great attention to their dreams and visions. There are stories too of warriors doing battle with supernatural fiends, such as the battle between Grettir and Glam, in the *Saga of Grettir the Strong*. Elsewhere we find that the priests of Freyja sensed when she was present within a decorated wagon. When this was paraded around the district, no disputes could continue. Finally, it was taken to a lake to be washed and the slaves who had performed this service were then executed. This is all a highly ceremonial form of magic, known as *galdr*, although it also relies on intuition.

The Oseburg wagon from Norway

Galdr magic can be quite imitative in the way it works, for example, writing an illness down on a piece of paper and then destroying it, with the intention of getting rid of the illness too. Taking that to a more elaborate level, there was a way of cursing someone known as the niding pole (from Old Norse *nidhstong*). A pole with a curse or ritual insult is left outside the victim's door, during the night. Sometimes it is topped with the head or skull of an animal, such as a horse. I would surmise that anyone finding such an item confronting them in the morning would be disturbed, whether they believed in magic or not! So something disturbing passes a feeling on to its victim. There is a tale of a bad king being driven out of his land by a powerful magician setting up a niding pole on the shore, facing landwards. It was considered bad luck to moor the Viking dragonships with their fearsome dragon figureheads facing a friend's land, as they would scare or insult the *landvattir* (land spirits). Some ships had detachable figureheads. On a practical note, having your ship facing down the beach for a quick getaway made sense as well!

The Valknut, found on some Odin orientated memorial stones, possibly symbolising the nine interconnected worlds

TAUFR MAGIC

A primary source of magic has to be the runes, though and the carving of runes (by one termed a *vitki*) is sometimes referred to as *Taufr*, i.e. Talismatic magic. One can see the enigmatic reference to the runic 'nine lays of power' detailed in the Havamal, which has verses about runes dulling the blades of enemies, deflecting their arrows or magic, loosing the shackles of prisoners, gaining a woman or calming an angry sea. Not all that would be of much practical use today, but it begs the important question, what is magic?

MAGICAL ETHICS AND PRECAUTIONS

From the myths we can see that some types of magic are not common to all gods and goddesses. Loki borrows Freyja's falcon-feather cloak to fly and Thor is not ashamed to ask the witch Groa to try to remove the whetstone fragment from his head. Someone once defined magic as bending natural forces to one's will. I would add that, as we are part of a nature religion, if we are in tune with

the natural world, then we must be part of it and be part of its inherent forces, bending with them. There is nothing more magic for me than seeing a delicate plant forcing its way up through a crack in the concrete to flower. It knows its will and is doing it. One of the prime aspects of many forms of magic is to really know your own will (for which you really need to know yourself) and then to project it. That is not a *carte blanche* to do what ever you want, since a person in tune with him or herself is rarely destructive, coercive or malicious. Some people define magic in two parts, higher and lower, where the higher part corresponds to knowing and changing the self and the lower to mundane workings such as healing others or improving situations.

How you work magic will be up to you and your personal background and preferences. Whatever you do, think it through first. It is better to do nothing than do the wrong thing and whenever you use magic you are interfering, even if it is with the best of intentions. Each spell you cast will have consequences, both immediate and as a knock-on effect. (Think back to the imagery of the Web of the Wyrd, where one tug on a thread causes the whole to vibrate.) You must consider whether what you are doing is truly useful in the long term, or will produce only a short-term gain. Let me give you a couple of examples.

Consider someone who has injured his wrist. The obvious practical thing to do is to get him to seek conventional medical advice and treatment. Magic should be a last resort, not a first response. Having had it bandaged, he comes to you for relief from some of the pain. You could perform a healing spell over it, maybe for example chanting/writing *laguz* or *beorth*, two runes associated with healing. But stop and think first! If the pain is relieved, will he then use the hand, instead of resting it, causing longer-term problems? After all, pain is often nature's way of getting us to stop doing harmful things to ourselves. Also, what if you think of the injury as being there for a purpose? It might prevent the injured person from playing tennis tomorrow, and thus not being introduced to the man who will swindle him out of his savings. See what I mean by knock-on effects? That is not to say you should not perform healing spells, but you might check what the recipient is going to do on feeling better

and put the onus on the person to ask you for a spell, rather than you take responsibility for laying it on him or her.

Let's look at another popular area of magic, that connected with romance. Suppose a young woman came to you asking for a bit of magical help in getting together with that good-looking, unattached guy she sees at the bus stop. Let's imagine you make a powerful ritual to bring them together. It works and they get married. A few months into the marriage, the woman discovers she is married to a wife beater. Now, what sort of magic have you worked? Certainly the intention was good, but the trouble with wishes and magic is that you do not always quite know what you are asking for. Was it fair to work against the man's natural actions, i.e. not approching her himself, thus taking away his choice in the matter? The popular images of black and white magic are misleading – most of it is in various hues of grey. If you worried about every consequence, you would not work magic at all, which some would say is preferable. However, with such an exciting and powerful tool at our disposal it is hard to resist the temptation to use it and I think the main safeguard must be to examine your motivations closely beforehand.

Of course, that is not the only precaution you must take whilst doing magic. Just as a professional electrician always protects himself from the electricity, and creates a safe working space, so must you. This is usually achieved by creating a sacred space in which to work. Only people and objects which you trust are allowed there and protection is requested from the deities and natural elements and spirits. Usually, the space is a circle, but there is no reason why it cannot be another shape. The *Ve* sacred enclosures of the Norse and Saxon peoples are believed to have been square. They had a rule about not coming into it armed, although they must have allowed at least one knife for sacrificing and carving an animal, which they frequently did as part of their rituals. These were known as *blots*, possibly in connection with the word 'blood', which was sprinkled all around the area and on the participants. Sometimes individuals built temples, such as Hrafnkel, the priest of Frey, who according to the Icelandic saga made many sacrifices, giving half his treasures to Frey. There were priestesses, too, who were probably more associated with Frey's sister Freyja. Some of these certainly worked in partnership, such as Thorthur Freysgothi (Frey's priest) and his sister who was known as Thurithur Hofgytha (temple priestess) of Freysnes, Iceland, who are referred to in Landnamabok, the Book of Settlements. You will notice that they are given the titles *gothi* and *gytha* (priest and priestess) which we most associate with more formal galdr magic, but the Goddess Freyja who they serve is said to be the bringer of the more shamanic seidr magic. This demonstrates how then, like today, there are no clear boundary lines concerning roles and which magic they use.

Ritual dancing figure detail from Sutton Hoo helmet

Ritual magic

Ritual magic can take many different forms and it is up to you how you perform it. There is no right or wrong way, only what feels appropriate for you. Some people like to plan rituals in advance and try to always do certain actions the same way. I always try to teach my pupils to make definite physical ritual actions to complement their definite thoughts. If you are presenting a Thorshammer to hallow something, hold it firm and make clear movements. You are not waving a banana about! If you look at Anglo Saxon verse

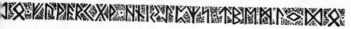

charms they do not ask for something to be done. They are that positive they say it has been done, already. The magician is confident that the stolen property is being returned, or the cows are giving more milk even as they speak!

Others prefer to rely upon the inspiration of the moment, rather than the pre-planned ritual, although this is more prone to mistakes. You might like to do quiet meditative pathworkings, runic carving and speak whispered words or you might want to dance (like the figure in the Sutton Hoo helmet illustrated), chant runes at the top of your voice and beat drums loud enough to wake the dead. If your choice falls towards the latter be warned – however far you get away from civilisation, sound carries through a wood at night and you might find yourself summoning the police to your circle instead of the hoped-for deity! I never summon anything myself – I believe one should have the good manners to ask politely. It is a matter of what attitude one has towards the deities. Norse Tradition does not teach a craven attitude though, as the myths show gods and goddesses who appreciate fierce independence rather than cowering timidity, so I guess kneeling and sycophancy are out, as far as our religion is concerned.

PRACTICE

Try to create a simple spell. There are plenty of books giving step-by-step instructions, but the Norse Tradition teaches independence and individual self-sufficiency, so try to invent your own. It will be just as valid as anything you can read elsewhere, but will have the additional potency of being personalised and understood by you. To get you started, here are a few elements you might like to incorporate: burning candles and incense; marking out your sacred space with a staff, wand, sword or whatever; chanting or writing runes; making up a poem or song to sing; setting up a rhythm with claps, stamps, rattles or drums; preparing some food or drink to be consumed as part of the magic. I am sure you can think of many more original elements of your own.

RecommenDeD reADING

Fries, Jan, *Seidways*, Mandrake, 1996

Gundarsson, Kveldulf, *Teutonic Magic*, Llewellyn, 1994

Harner, Michael, *The Way of the Shaman*, Harper and Row, 1986

McGrath, Sheena, *Asyniur: Women's Mysteries in the Northern Tradition*, Capall Bann, 1997

McNallen, Stephen A., *Rituals of Asatru*, Vols 1–3, World Tree, 1992

Rodrigues, Louis J., *Anglo Saxon Verse Charms, Maxims and Heroic Legends*, Anglo Saxon, 1993

Thorrson, Edred, *Futhark: A handbbok of rune magic*, Weiser, 1991; *A Book of Troth*, 1989, *The 9 Doors of Midgard*, 1991, *Rune Might*, 1994, *Northern Magic*, 1992, all by Llewellyn

8

SOME SIMPLE
RITUALS

*In Chapter 11 I shall give you some points of contact to network with
other members of the Norse Tradition. If there is an Odinist hearth
group near where you live, you may be able to join in some of their
activities and get a feeling for what works for you. Do not join a group
you are unhappy with. It is better to take a solo path than be pushed
along a route with which you feel uncomfortable. Do not dabble in
magic. You wouldn't dabble in brain surgery and this is just as
important. Prepare properly and safeguard yourself. Sooner or later
you will have to work by yourself (or with a partner) anyway, whether
you are part of a hearth or not.*

I would like to give you a starting point from which to build your
rituals. It will be one of several you can find, including some in the
recommended reading list at the end of this chapter. The rituals
I will suggest are not definitive. They are there for you to add to,
edit or whatever until you reach your own personal plan. Let's start
with a sequence that you will need, in one form or another, for
every ritual. As we are a nature religion I assume all rituals are held
outdoors unless it is impractical to do so.

Locate North (with a compass if necessary) and set up your altar
space there. A tree stump, box or cloth on the ground will do. Be
still and quiet and concentrate on being in tune with your
surroundings. When ready, take a staff or other tool and trace the
outline of a circular (or rectangular, triangular, etc.) working area
with it on the ground, big enough for all you wish to do and to
contain all present. I personally start in the East and work clockwise
like the sun, but you may have another preference. Next, purify the

circle with some water, sprinkled from a bowl with a branch. You could say something like 'I create this sacred space and purify it, so that all that happens within it will be honourable and good.' If you are working with other people, involve them too, sharing out the various duties.

You might like to light candles or incense at some point. If you are working at night, set candles in jars or lanterns, hung on poles driven in the ground. That way you do not have to crawl around the ground to read the words. (Of course, it is better if you can learn the words by heart or be confident enough to improvise them on the spot, so that scripts are not required.)

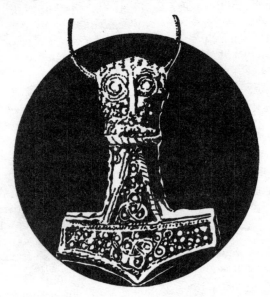

Thorshammer (Mjollnir) pendant

Next, make an invocation to each of the cardinal points. This can be the sign of Thor's hammer (an inverted T), drawn in the air, together with appropriate invitations to the deities and/or elemental forces you associate with each quarter. Alternatively you may hold a ceremonial hammer in the air. Throughout the world, many cultures associate

the same elements with specific directions: East–Air, South–Fire, West–Water, North–Earth. For example, your invocations could be:

East: 'Guardians of Austri. Welcome Odin and Frigga, and the spirit of Hraevelgr, whose wings direct the winds.'

South: 'Guardians of Sudri. Welcome Thor and Sif, Balder and Nanna, and the spirit of Surt's fire.'

West: 'Guardians of Westri. Welcome Heimdall and the spirit of Aegir's watery sea.'

North: 'Guardians of Nordri. Welcome Frey and Freyja and the spirit of Fjorgyn and Erce of the earth.'

(The Guardian names are taken from the elemental elves given in the mythology.)

Finally, from the **centre** you could make a general greeting: 'I welcome all here, be they Gods, spirits or humans. Let none take offence as we try to concentrate our good wishes into the centre of this sacred space. May all that attend here guard and protect the sanctity of this place and not leave it until the rituals end. May this be a gateway to the nine worlds of Yggdrasil and our work be as fruitful as Frigga. Let no one disturb a place hallowed with Thor the Thunderer's protection.' (All make hammer sign.)

You can now get on with whatever specific ritual you are working that night, be it a baby naming, initiation, handfast wedding or funeral. (I'd advise against all four at the same event!) At some point you should have some food and drink. This is usually towards the end and can consist of mead, beer, juice or wine with bread, cakes meat or fruit. It is traditional within all parts of the Northern Tradition to do this and very often the drink is shared from a drinking horn. You should bless the food and drink before distribution and save a portion to be left as an offering back to the earth that provided it. Suitable blessings might be 'We thank Sif for the fruit of her golden hair. May none of us be hungry in the company of another.' And 'We thank Kvasir for his lifeblood preserved in this mead. May none of us ever be thirsty in the company of another.' (Sif's hair is a poetic kenning for corn and the myths tell of mead coming from Kvasir's death.)

At the end of the night's work you must close down the space properly. It will help to close you down as well, so that you are not wide awake and psychically very aware at four in the morning! Sacred spaces left open and abandoned act as beacons for all sorts of dubious characters and are a menace to others. Most people reverse the process they start with, so you could go back to the cardinal points in reverse order (East, North, West and South) and say:

'Thank you all for your help and aid within the ritual. Until we meet again we bid you *waes hael*!'

(*Waes hael* is an Anglo Saxon phrase translating as 'be hale, or healthy'. It is often used by Heathens as a greeting or farewell phrase. The word for a type of seasonal song, 'wassail' derives from it.)

So there you have the framework for an opening or closing, which you can simplify, elaborate and customise. It is important to try to stimulate all the senses in a ritual. In the ritual described you can see that there were sights (candles), smells (incense), sounds (words), tastes (food and drink) and touch (the sprinkling of water). I think it is important to involve everyone present, rather than have 'expert' doers and passive 'watchers'.

PRACTICE

1 Customise the opening and closing ritual above for your own tastes and use.
2 Construct a ritual to go into the middle of it. It could be for a funeral, handfasting or any other purpose, but try to utilise all senses. It could be a specific anniversary celebration, such as the Yule or Summer Solstice. Perhaps you could incorporate a folk song or dance or even make up a ritual drama, with parts for everyone, from one of the myths you have read. Do not forget that you can use runes as well, to chant, scribe or as body postures. If actions or words are to be repeated, three and nine are the numbers of major magical significance within the tradition. You might get some additional ideas from some of the recommended books, both in this and the previous chapters. Certainly try to incorporate any details from the

myths and sagas that are relevant, for example, in the Lay of Thrym when Thor pretends to be a bride, he is offered food and drink, wears a veil and has a hammer placed in his lap. These are all details you can use in putting together a handfast wedding ceremony. If you were planning a funeral rite, the story of Balder's ship burial contains detail about nine maidens (possibly the wave maiden daughters of Aegir) throwing blue scarves into the air, something quite easily incorporated into a modern rite.

Recommended reading

Conway, D.J., *Norse Magic*, Llewellyn
Fitch, Ed, *Rites of Odin*, Llewellyn, 1990
Fries, Jan, *Visual Magic*, 1992 and *Helrunar*, 1993, both Mandrake
Tyson, Donald, *Rune Magic*, Llewellyn, 1988

a seasonal cycle

As a nature religion, the Norse Tradition draws upon the phenomena of the natural world and its cycle of birth, life and death for its seasonal festivals. Most of us are used to thinking in terms of four seasons and it is not too hard to draw parallels with human development; birth in spring, maturity in summer, old age in autumn and death in winter. Thus, death is a part of the life cycle and new birth follows it.

Most of the Teutonic derived tribes seem to have divided the year into two, with spring as a part of summer and autumn as part of winter. This differs from the Celtic Pagan festival cycle, which for them starts at Samhain on 31 October. The Norse year starts at the Yule solstice, around 21 December, which is known as Mother's Night. No one really knows whether this refers to biological mothers, earth mother, Disir goddesses or even all three, but it is a great time for a feast and fire to dispel the gloomy cold of winter and observe the sun starting to get slightly stronger again. Having said all that, you will often find those of the Norse Tradition joining their friends of other Pagan paths in celebrating some of the dates on the Celtic calendar. Firstly, some were probably common to both cultures, but, anyway, we Vikings always appreciate having a good time!

Many people of our tradition use the solstices and full moons as regular, natural markers for their meetings and rituals. Many have also, in recent years, designated specific days to commemorate particular aspects of our faith. I have shown these in the accompanying table, together with some moon month names used by many in place of the Roman derived calendar. Some take this further by making the spelling of days closer to the original divine

connections, i.e. Sun-day, Moon-day, Tiws-day, Wodens-day, Thors-day, Friggas-day, Sataere-day. You will also find that some folk deliberately use a different year number, which is 250 years older than the Christian one. So 1998 becomes 2248 RE, the RE standing for Runic Era.

Of course, there may be other dates which are significant for you, which you want to make part of your annual calendar. If you become involved in carrying out one of the traditional folk customs, this will become an important stage of the year to you. Some people celebrate the anniversary of the first meeting of their hearth group or their handfast wedding. Others make a point of remembering the day they first worked a ritual or were initiated into a group. The point is to have a regular calendar of festivals that mean something to you, not to celebrate someone else's imposed list.

It is worth remembering that our ancestors did not go in for elaborate, fixed-date, calendars. They were far more likely to judge that spring had arrived by the buds sprouting on a particular plant, than because it was a certain date. In the accompanying table I have shown some modern month names given by Odinists against both their Romanised equivalents and the Anglo Saxon names written down by Bede, together with what he thought they signified. I have also indicated some days celebrated by some, but not all, of the Norse Tradition.

One can make some specific connections with the mythology and the seasons. For example, the second half of Freygerda's name means frozen field. So in the story of *Skirnir's Journey*, where Frey the fertility God falls in love and seeks to woo her, one might interpret their union as spring. At the other end of summer, when Loki cuts Sif's beautiful hair and has to replace it with spun gold, it is usually assumed to signify the cutting of the golden corn of harvest. Similarly, when the God of goodness and light, Balder is sent to Hel, it can be interpreted as the dying of the sun in winter, although one can view it in other ways. The sun and moon have a special place in the Norse creation myths, as they do in most cultures, but does the reference to the ravening wolves Skoll and Hati, chasing them to gobble them up refer to eclipses? I am sure as you read the mythology, you can find many more apparent connections with the natural world.

Norse Tradition calendar

Asatru	Bede	Roman	Date	Festival	Theme
Snowmoon	Yule/Guili	Jan	17	Charming the plough	Labour
Horningmoon	Solmonath (cakes)	Feb	2	Disir	Imbolc
Horningmoon	Solmonath	Feb	14	Vali	Family
Lentingmoon	Hrethmonath (Goddess)	Mar	20	Summer Finding	Ostara
Ostara	Eostre (Goddess)	Apr	23	Sigurd	Homeland
Ostara	Eostre	Apr	30	Walpurgisnacht	May eve customs
Merrymoon	Thrimilci (3 milkings)	May	22	Ragnar Lodbrok	Viking hero
Merrymoon	Thrimilci	May	30	Vanir	Vanir
Fallowmoon	Litha (Double size month of Moon)	Jun	8	Lindisfarne Day	1st raid
Fallowmoon		Jun	21	Midsummer	Balder
Fallowmoon	Litha	Jun	24	Aesir	Aesir
Haymoon	Litha	Jul	15	Alfar	Elves
Haymoon	Litha	Jul	22	Sleipnir	Life
Haymoon	Litha	Jul	30	Perchta Mannus	Lughnasagh
Harvestmoon	Weodmonath	Aug	24	Runes	The mind
Harvestmoon	(Weeds)	Aug	26	Harvest	Harvest
Sheddingmoon	Halegmonath (Offerings)	Sep	9	Herman of Cherusci	Memories
Sheddingmoon	Halegmonath	Sep	23	Winter-Finding	Harvest end
Huntingmoon	Wintirfylith (1st full moon of winter)	Oct	12	Hengest	Settlement
Huntingmoon	Wintirfylith	Oct	approx 19–20	Winter Sat & Sun	Winter
Huntingmoon	Wintirfylith	Oct	31	Hallowe'en	Samhain
Fogmoon	Blotmonath	Nov	1	Heimdall	God
Fogmoon	(Sacrifice)	Nov	11	Einherjar	War hero
Fogmoon	Blotmonath	Nov	23	Wayland Smith	Folk hero
Wolfmoon	Yule/Guili	Dec	1	Ullr	God
Wolfmoon	Yule/Guili	Dec	21	Mother's Night	Mid-Winter

Sif and her hair of golden corn

PRACTICE

1 What dates are significant to you? Why not make up your own personal religious calendar? You may want to refer to some of the books at the end of Chapter 5.
2 Can you find a myth that appears to say something about the natural world?

RECOMMENDED READING

Trubshaw, Bob, *Grimr's Year*, Heart of Albion, 1991

10

the hard
questions

The Norse Tradition has so much to offer as a spiritual path, but it obviously has its detractors, both within and outside the world of Paganism. One of its most obvious problems is the association of Nazis with both runes and parts of the mythology. This is a problem faced by many religions. Anything that is a powerful stirrer of emotions will be misused by others to further their own cause. If, however, we ban the use of runes on the basis that Nazis used the double sigil as a symbol for the SS, etc., then we allow them to have won.

I believe it is more appropriate to seize back and reclaim such symbols for their rightful use. After all, Christians did not stop using the crucifix after its adoption by the Ku-Klux-Klan. The Nazis pushed an ideology of a pure Aryan master race. If you have examined the historical evidence connected with Chapter 2, you will find that the Northern European peoples are a mixture of Saxon, Jute, Frisian, Dane, Jewish, Norman and many other ethnic groups, and the idea of a pure race becomes laughable. However, that does not stop some racists from trying to use those discredited theories to bolster their own paranoid inadequacies. Unfortunately, some of them have joined or even help to run certain Odinist organisations and do a great discredit to our movement. It is ironic that the Nazis closed down most esoteric organisations and Hitler apparently paid his Catholic Church tax until the day he died! In Chapter 11 are the addresses of a couple of UK organisations I believe to be free of such evil influences.

Frank's Casket, showing warriors

The other uninformed criticism levelled at the Norse Tradition is that it cannot be right to follow a tradition that was renowned for rape and pillage. I would argue that most of the world's religions have found their roots in ancient, violent civilisations. One could also argue that they continue to flourish in a modern, more violent world, despite their teachings! The Vikings were no better or worse than many of their contemporaries, but were the subject of influential writing by the churchmen they attacked. Much of their beautiful artistry is wrongly attributed today as Celtic (who were not the only group to design complicated knotwork jewellery) and their achievements in exploration, poetry, democratic government and women's rights are conveniently ignored.

Of course, we have to adapt the ancient beliefs for our modern life just as other religions have learnt by experience to do. Human or animal sacrifice is no longer necessary and it is impractical to have

a ship burial today. However, we can carry on those historic positive qualities of respect for the natural world, loyalty to one's tribe and living an honourable life. As we have seen in Chapter 7, magic in itself is neutral. It is how we use it that makes it good or bad. If we live an honourable life, we would not normally consider using the black magic that we might be capable of, because it would lessen our reputation. That might be the ethical root of why people of the Norse Tradition do not use 'black' magic, rather than the more karmic ideal of the wiccan 'An it harm none.'

That leads to another question: Are we of the Norse Tradition witches? Certainly by the more modern definitions favoured by initiatory movements, such as Gardnerian or Alexandian Wicca, we are not. We do not have a formalised degree system or chain of initiation. However, the older definition of a witch is simply that of a person who does magic, within the framework of their Pagan beliefs.

A niding pole

So every witch is a Pagan, but Pagans who do not try to use magic are not witches. If you attempt magic within the Odinist path, then I believe that makes you a witch, if you want to be called one. Certainly, it is still an emotive word for some but I am happy to be labelled a witch. Despite both Odin and Thor seeking their aid within the mythology it is an uncommon term within our tradition.

All this means that some of the hardest questions we have to answer about our beliefs come from ourselves, rather than from outside. How do we live ethically, on a day-to-day basis? Where does our respect for the law give way to our right of defence, and how do we interpret the meanings of the ancient texts in our personal lives? How do we label ourselves and regard the gods and goddesses, as spiritual beings or extensions of our own psyche? Living the Norse Tradition is much harder than reading about it!

PRACTICE

1 Imagine a favourite aunt has written to you. She has heard that you have begun to 'dabble in the occult' and are 'taking an unhealthy interest in Vikings'. She is elderly, and occasionally goes to church. Compose a diplomatic, but honest letter to allay her fears.

2 Some towns have moots nowadays – Pagan discussion groups that meet in pubs or houses, with people of different paths attending. If you can get to one, try to get a discussion going about Norse Tradition, or an aspect of it. If they have lectures, perhaps you could even offer to give a short talk. Be ready to defend or explain your beliefs, without attacking the differing ideas of others.

RECOMMENDED READING

Anon, trans. G.N. Garmonsway, *The Anglo Saxon Chronicle*,
  Everyman, 1954
King, Bernard, *Ultima Thule: The Vanished Northern Homeland*,
  Rune Gild UK, 1992
Simek, Rudolph, trans. Angela Hall, *Dictionary of Northern
  Mythology*, D.S. Brewer, 1996
Whitelock, Dorothy, *The Beginnings of English Society*, Pelican, 1977
Yeowell, John, *Odinism and Christianity under the Third Reich*,
  Odinic Rite: Edda, 1993

where to go from here

If you have by now decided to follow a Northern Tradition path, you might be wondering how to progress, having read this book. First and foremost, you will have to decide whether you wish to specialise in particular aspects. Do you want to explore the ways of the Anglo Saxons or Norse? Do you want to train for a gothi/gytha priest/priestess role, or do you see yourself in a more shamanistic role, as a female volva or male shaman. Also, you must consider whether you want to dedicate yourself to one particular god or goddess rather than a whole pantheon.

There are also the warrior cults to consider. The best known of these is the *berserker*, or bear shirt cult, whose adherents emulated a bear and whipped themselves up into a fighting frenzy. Similar in nature are the Ulfhednar wolf warrior cult. There is also one brief reference to Chati, which seems to refer to warriors with a cat totem and the Svinfylking who related closely to the sacred boar of Frey. (There are references to boar cults amongst both Saxons and Scandinavians and at least two boar's head helmets have been found in England.) Not much is known about the practices or rites of any of these warrior cults, but they may well be worth exploring if you are a fighter in spirit. The Saxon hero Hereward the Wake, who fought a guerilla war against the Normans, is credited with killing a Norwegian bear and called upon Danish berserkers, with whom he had made friends, to aid him in his fenland fight.

Boar's head helmet associated with Frey

PRACTICE

Go out to a quiet natural place and meditate on what you have read in this book. Decide whether this path is for you and, if so, whether you want a specialised role within it. Decide whether you identify especially with any particular deity. Make a personal oath about what you intend to do and ask the help of all the gods and goddesses.

useful addresses

You might like to try to contact others of the Norse Tradition to exchange ideas, join together in a hearth or be taught. Here are the addresses of some organisations to help you. In each case, send a stamped self-addressed envelope for your reply, or international reply coupons.

Odinshof, BM: Tercel, London, WC1N 3XX

Ring of Troth UK, BM: Aswynn, London, WC1N 3XX

The Pagan Federation, BM: 7097, London, WC1N 3XX

The last of these is not an Odinist organisation, but provides information and contacts on all paths of Paganism for its members, runs magazines, moots and conferences as well as publishing the Northern Tradition Information Pack.
Website http://www.paganfed.demon.co.uk

There is a specialist Anglo Saxon historical society, which is not specifically heathen but is very helpful with all things of that era. In modern language they are known as the English Companions, but their proper title is:

Da Engliscan Gesidas, BM Box 4336, London WC1N 3XX. They have a website at:

http://www.kami.demon.co.uk/gesithas/gesith.htm

There is some interesting material, too, on:

http://www.anglo-saxon.demon.co.uk
http://www.personal.u-net.com/~midgard/

Elsewhere around the world, there are many more Asatru organisations and publishers, particularly in the United States. Inevitably, the list becomes out of date as soon as it is published, but this gives you a starting point to try to find others of a like mind. I cannot vouch for all that I have listed, as I do not know them personally. As always, when making new friends be careful, and do not be drawn into anything you are uncomfortable with. If you have access to the Internet you can visit dozens of sites run by individual hearths as well as organisations. The biggest listing of links I have found is on the first site named here:

Irmisul Aettir   http://www.eskimo.com/~valkyrie/

Ring of Troth (USA) and *Idunna* magazine, PO Box 25637, Tempe, AZ 85285, USA
http://www.netusa.net/~jmr/troth.html

The Asatru Folk Assembly, PO Box 445, Nevada City, CA 95959, USA   http://www.runestone.org/dir.html

Asatru Alliance, *Vor Tru* magazine and World Tree Publications, PO Box 961, Payson, AZ 85547, USA

The Rune Gild, PO Box 7622, University Station, Austin, TX 78713, USA

American Vinland Association, 537 Jones St 2154, San Francisco, CA 94102, USA   http://vinland.org/heathen/ava/

Hrafnar, c/o Diana L Paxson, Box 5521, Berkeley, CA 94705, USA
http://vinland.org/heathen/hrafnar

Uncle Thorrs magazine, The Trollwise Press, PO Box 080437, Staten Island, NY 10308-0005, USA

Eagles Reach/Aernfolk, c/o Ymir Thunarsson, PO Box 327, Roanoke, TX 76262, USA   http://members.tripod.com/~aernfol/index-2html

Heritage and Tradition, CP 244, SUCC. P.A.T., Montreal, Quebec H1B 5K3, Canada

Bifrost Kindred, Suite 131, 5642-23 Ave, Edmonton, AB T6L 6NZ, Canada   http://www.geocities.com/Athens/Forum/2716/

Icelandic Asatru Association, PO Box 1423, 123 Reykjavik, Iceland

Renewal **magazine**, PO Box 4333, University of Melbourne, Victoria 3052, Australia

Folkvangr Hearth (Australasia)
http://zurix.apana.org.au/asatru/hearth.htm

Assembly of Elder Troth, PO Box 331X, Leumeah, NSW 2560, Australia   http://203.15.68.48/Pagan/AET.html

De Noordse Traditie, Postbus 1292, 2302, BG Leiden, Netherlands
http://www1.tip.nl/~t887876

Bifrost, Norway   http://www.bifrost.no/enghome.html

Gladsaxe Blodtgilde, Trongaardsvej 44, 2800 Lyngby, Danmark
http://www.lyngbyes.dk

Sveriges Asatrosamfund, Box 4001, 13604 Haninge, Sweden
Tel: 08 7412101   http://www.asatro.a.se/

Natveket For Nordisk Sed, Sweden,
http://www.solace.mh.se/~alpha/nordsed.htm

Rabenclan, Germany   http://www.rabenclan.de/

Heidenkreis, Postfach 630317, 22313 Hamburg, Germany
http://members.aol.com/ThingHH/frame.html

Organise your own hearth

If you cannot find an existing hearth group to join in your area it can be rewarding to organise several beginners to meet and learn together, rather than relying on an 'expert' to teach you. After all, our tradition teaches us to be self-sufficient and independent. Both Odinshof and Ring of Troth can advise you on how best to do this and provide you with correspondence course training and contacts in your area who may be potential recruits. My advice is to start small and look for some practical commitment to the path in those who seek to join. It is better to have a small dedicated hearth than a large one with a floating population of people with separate agendas. Agree a written set of ground rules and objectives at the start, so people know where they stand.

Recommended reading

Now that you have made some decisions about how you plan to continue, you may want to refer to the recommended reading from the different chapters to learn about specific topics relative to the path you have chosen. Remember, though, that there is a limit to how much you can learn from books. At some stage you must actually do things and learn from the experience! I will, however, finish with two fictional books that did not fit into any particular chapter, but are well worth reading. I wish you an interesting and rewarding quest.

Bates, Brian, *The Way of the Wyrd*, Arrow, 1987
Tolkien, J.R.R., *Lord of the Rings*, HarperCollins, 1992

Other titles in this series

Astral Projection 0 340 67418 0 **£5.99** Is it possible for the soul to leave the body at will? In this book the traditional techniques used to achieve astral projection are described in a simple, practical way, and Out of the Body and Near Death Experiences are also explored.

Astrology 0 340 72080 8 **£5.99** An exploration of how astrology helps us to understand ourselves and other people. Learn how to draw up and interpret a horoscope.

Astrology and Health 0 340 70518 3 **£5.99** This book explains simply the symbolic richness of the zodiac signs and how they can illuminate our experience of health.

Becoming Prosperous 0 340 69773 3 **£5.99** A guide to how *anyone* can feel and become more prosperous by focusing on state of mind and conscious thought. Practical exercises help readers develop personal strategies to become more prosperous, both financially and emotionally.

Chakras 0 340 62082 X **£5.99** The body's energy centres, the chakras, can act as gateways to healing and increased self-knowledge. This book shows you how to work with chakras in safety and with confidence.

Channelling 0 340 70472 1 **£5.99** Channelling is the process by which ancient knowledge and wisdom are tapped and reclaimed for the enlightenment and enrichment of life in the present. This book offers simple techniques to become channels of awareness.

Chinese Horoscopes 0 340 64804 X **£5.99** In the Chinese system of horoscopes, the year of birth is all-important. *Chinese Horoscopes for beginners* tells you how to determine your own Chinese horoscope, what personality traits you are likely to have, and how your fortunes may fluctuate in years to come.

Dowsing 0 340 60882 X **£5.99** People all over the world have used dowsing since the earliest times. This book shows how to start dowsing – what to use, what to dowse, and what to expect when subtle energies are detected.

Dream Interpretation 0 340 60150 7 **£5.99** This fascinating introduction to the art and science of dream interpretation explains how to unravel the meaning behind dream images to interpret your own and other people's dreams.

Earth Mysteries 0 340 70516 7 **£5.99** What can we learn from observing the earth and the remains of our prehistoric ancestors? Explore ley lines, earth energies, astro-archaeology and sacred landscapes to expand your consciousness and achieve a better perspective on existence.

Enlightenment 0 340 70515 9 **£5.99** Learn how you can experience primary enlightenment through tried-and-tested exercises which offer the tools to help you to find your own unique truth.

Feng Shui 0 340 62079 X **£5.99** This beginner's guide to the ancient art of luck management will show you how to increase your good fortune and well-being by harmonising your environment with the natural energies of the earth.

Freeing Your Intuition 0 340 71149 3 **£5.99** Develop awareness of your intuition and make your own good fortune, increase your creative output and learn to recognise what you *know*, not just what you think.

Gems and Crystals 0 340 60883 8 **£5.99** For centuries gems and crystals have been used as an aid to healing and meditation. This guide tells you all you need to know about choosing, keeping and using stones to increase your personal awareness and improve your well-being.

The Goddess 0 340 68390 2 **£5.99** This book traces the development, demise and rebirth of the Goddess, looking at the worship of Her and retelling myths from all over the world.

Graphology 0 340 60625 8 **£5.99** Graphology, the science of interpreting handwriting to reveal personality, is now widely accepted and used throughout the world. This introduction will enable you to make a comprehensive analysis of your own and other people's handwriting to reveal the hidden self.

The Healing Powers of Plants 0 340 71148 5 **£5.99** Plants and herbs can be used to enhance everyday life through aromatherapy, herbalism, homoeopathy and colour therapy. Their power can be used in cosmetics, meditation and home decoration.

Herbs for Magic and Ritual 0 340 67415 6 **£4.99** This book looks at the well-known herbs and the stories attached to them. There is information on the use of herbs in essential oils and incense, and on their healing and magical qualities.

I Ching 0 340 62080 3 **£5.99** The roots of *I Ching* or the *Book of Changes* lie in the time of the feudal mandarin lords of China, but its traditional wisdom is still relevant today. Using the original poetry in its translated form, this introduction traces its history, survival and modern-day applications.

Interpreting Signs and Symbols 0 340 68827 0 **£5.99** The history of signs and symbols is traced in this book from their roots to the modern age. It also examines the way psychiatry uses symbolism, and the significance of doodles.

The Language of Flowers 0 340 69781 4 **£5.99** Flowers can and do heal us, both emotionally and physically, with their smell and their beauty. By looking at these areas, together with superstitions associated with flowers and their links with New Age subjects, the author gives advice on how to enhance your life with flowers.

Love Signs 0 340 64805 8 **£5.99** This is a practical introduction to the astrology of romantic relationships. It explains the different roles played by each of the planets, focusing particularly on the position of the Moon at the time of birth.

The Magic and Mystery of Trees 0 340 70494 2 **£5.99** This book explores the many meanings of trees, from myth and folklore through ritual and seasonal uses to their 'spiritual essence' and esoteric meanings.

Meditation 0 340 64835 X **£5.99** This beginner's guide gives simple, clear instructions to enable you to start meditating and benefiting from this ancient mental discipline immediately. The text is illustrated throughout by full-colour photographs and line drawings.

Mediumship 0 340 68009 1 **£5.99** Whether you want to become a medium yourself, or simply understand what mediumship is about, this book will give you the grounding to undertake a journey of discovery into the spirit realms.

The Moon and You 0 340 64836 8   £5.99   The phase of the Moon when you were born radically affects your personality. This book looks at nine lunar types – how they live, love, work and play, and provides simple tables to find out the phase of your birth.

Numerology 0 340 59551 5   £5.99   Despite being scientifically based, numerology requires no great mathematical talents to understand. This introduction gives you all the information you will need to understand the significance of numbers in your everyday life.

Numerology and Relationships 0 340 72450 1   £5.99   This guide takes you step by step through the hidden meanings behind the important numbers in your life to discover more about you, your compatibilities with others and the crucial relationships with your parents, partner and children.

Pagan Gods for Today's Man 0 340 69130 1   £5.99   Looking at ancient gods and old stories, this guide explores the social and psychological issues affecting the role of men today. In these pages men of all ages and persuasions can find inspiration.

Paganism 0 340 67013 4   £5.99   Pagans are true Nature worshippers who celebrate the cycles of life. This guide describes pagan festivals and rituals and takes a detailed look at the many forms of paganism practised today.

Palmistry 0 340 59552 3   £5.99   Palmistry is the oldest form of character reading still in use. This illustrated guide shows you exactly what to look for and how to interpret what you find.

Qabalah 0 340 67339 7   £5.99   The Qabalah is an ancient Jewish system of spiritual knowledge centred on the Tree of Life. This guide explains how it can be used in meditation and visualisation, and links it to the chakras, yoga, colour therapy, crystals, Tarot and numerology.

Reiki 0 340 72081 6   £5.99   In this book you will find advice on how to learn Reiki, its application and potential, and you will be shown an avenue of understanding of this simple, practical technique which offers pain relief through meditation and laying-on of hands.

Reincarnation and You 0 340 70517 5   £5.99   What happens to us after death? Here, you will find practical advice on using dreams, recurrent visions, déjà vu and precognition to access hidden parts of your consciousness which recall or anticipate past and future lives.

Runes 0 340 62081 1   £5.99   The power of the runes in healing and giving advice about relationships and life in general has been acknowledged since the time of the Vikings. This book shows how runes can be used in our technological age to increase personal awareness and stimulate individual growth.

Shamanism 0 340 68010 5   £5.99   Shamanic technique offers direct contact with Spirit, vivid self-knowledge and true kinship with plants, animals and the planet Earth. This book describes the shamanic way, the wisdom of the Medicine Wheel and power animals.

Some Traditional African Beliefs 0 340 70471 3   £5.99   Fortune telling and healing are two of the aspects of traditional African spiritual life looked at in this book. Exercises based on ancient beliefs show you how to use the environment to find ways to harmonise modern urban life in a practical way.

Spiritual Healing 0 340 67416 4 £5.99 All healing starts with self, and the Universal Power which makes this possible is available to everyone. In this book there are exercises, techniques and guidelines to follow which will enable you to heal yourself and others spiritually.

Star Signs 0 340 59553 1 £5.99 This detailed analysis looks at each of the star signs in turn and reveals how your star sign affects everything about you. This book shows you how to use this knowledge in your relationships and in everyday life.

Tantric Sexuality 0 340 68349 X £5.99 Tantric Buddhists use sex as a pleasurable path to enlightenment. This guide offers a radically different and exciting new dimension to sex, explaining practical techniques in a clear and simple way.

Tarot 0 340 59550 7 £5.99 Tarot cards have been used for many centuries. This guide gives advice on which sort to buy, where to get them and how to use them. The emphasis is on using the cards positively, as a tool for gaining self-knowledge, while exploring present and future possibilities.

Visualisation 0 340 65495 3 £5.99 This introduction to visualisation, a form of self-hypnosis widely used by Buddhists, will show you how to practise the basic techniques – to relieve stress, improve your health and increase your sense of personal well-being.

Witchcraft 0 340 67014 2 £5.99 This guide to the ancient religion based on Nature worship answers many of the questions and uncovers the myths and misconceptions surrounding witchcraft. Mystical rituals and magic are explained and there is advice for the beginner on how to celebrate the Sabbats.

Working With Colour 0 340 67011 8 £5.99 Colour is the medicine of the future. This book explores the energy of each colour and its significance, gives advice on how colour can enhance our well-being, and gives ideas on using colour in the home and garden.

Your Psychic Powers 0 340 67417 2 £5.99 Are you psychic? This book will help you find out by encouraging you to look more deeply within yourself. Psychic phenomena such as precognitive dreams, out of body travels and visits from the dead are also discussed in this ideal stepping stone towards a more aware you.

To order this series

All books in this series are available from bookshops or, in case of difficulty, can be ordered direct from the publisher. Prices and availability subject to change without notice. Send your order with your name and address to : Hodder & Stoughton Ltd, Cash Sales Department, Bookpoint, 39 Milton Park, Abingdon, OXON, OX14 4TD, UK. If you have a credit card you may order by telephone – 01235 831700.

Please enclose a cheque or postal order made payable to Bookpoint Ltd, allow the following for postage and packing: UK & BFPO: £1.00 for the first book, 50p for the second book and 30p for each additional book ordered up to a maximum charge of £3.00. OVERSEAS & EIRE: £2.00 for the first book, £1.00 for the second book and 50p for each additional book.

For sales in the following countries please contact:
UNITED STATES: Trafalgar Square (Vermont), Tel: 800 423 4525 (toll-free)
CANADA: General Publishing (Ontario), Tel: 445 3333
AUSTRALIA: Hodder & Stoughton (Sydney), Tel: 02 638 5299